Science Projects About
Chemistry

Science Projects About
Chemistry

Robert Gardner

● Science Projects ●

Enslow Publishers, Inc.
40 Industrial Road   PO Box 38
Box 398   Aldershot
Berkeley Heights, NJ 07922   Hants GU12 6BP
USA   UK
http://www.enslow.com

Library of Congress Cataloging-in-Publication Data

Gardner, Robert, 1929-
    Science projects about chemistry / by Robert Gardner.
        p. cm. — (Science projects)
    Includes bibliographical references and index.
    ISBN 0-89490-531-7
    1. Chemistry—Experiments—Juvenile literature. 2. Science
projects—Juvenile literature. [1. Chemistry—Experiments.
2. Experiments. 3. Science projects.] I. Title. II. Series:
Gardner, Robert, 1929–   Science projects.
QD38.G38   1994
540'.78—dc20   94-959
                                                          CIP
                                                          AC

Printed in the United States of America

10 9 8 7

To Our Readers: All Internet Addresses in this book were active and appropriate
when we went to press. Any comments or suggestions can be sent by e-mail to
Comments@enslow.com or to the address on the back cover.

Illustration Credits: Stephen F. Delisle

Cover Photo: © Stuart Simons, 1994

Contents

*appropriate for science fair project ideas

*appropriate for science fair project ideas

Introduction

This book is filled with science projects and experiments about chemistry. Most of the materials you will need to carry out these activities can be found in your home or school. Several of the experiments may require materials that you can buy in a supermarket, a hobby shop or a hardware store. You will need someone to help you with a few activities that require more than one pair of hands and, if any danger is involved, it will be indicated. It would be best if you work with friends or adults who enjoy experimenting as much as you do. In that way, you will both enjoy what you are doing.

Like a good scientist, you will find it useful to record your ideas, notes, data and anything you can conclude from your experiments in a notebook. By so doing, you can keep track of the information you gather and the conclusions you reach. It will allow you to refer back to other experiments you have done that may be useful to you in projects you will do later.

Chemists today assume that matter is made up of atoms and molecules. Atoms are the basic building blocks of elements such iron, carbon, aluminum, oxygen and hydrogen. These atoms cannot be broken down into simpler substances. Molecules are combinations of atoms. They make up the basic particles of compounds such as water, sugar, starch and carbon dioxide. Compounds can be broken down into the elements combined in their molecules. For example, water molecules consist of two atoms of hydrogen and one atom of oxygen. Thus, the compound water can be decomposed into two gases—hydrogen and oxygen. Since hydrogen and oxygen are elements, they cannot be further decomposed. They can recombine to form water, but they cannot be broken down into simpler substances. There is good evidence for believing that atoms and molecules exist, but in this book we will simply assume their existence.

Science Fairs

Some of the projects in this book may be appropriate for a science fair. Those projects are indicated with an asterisk (*). However, judges at such fairs do not reward projects or experiments that are simply copied from a book. For example, the fizzy reaction that occurs when vinegar is added to baking soda would probably not impress judges; however, a series of experiments designed to find what factors affect the rate of such a reaction would be likely to receive serious consideration. Science fair judges tend to reward creative thought and imagination. It's difficult to be creative or imaginative unless you are really interested in your project; consequently, it's wise to choose something that appeals to you. And before you jump into a project consider, too, your own talents and the cost of materials you will need.

If you decide to use a project found in this book for a science fair, you should find ways to modify or extend it. This should not be difficult because you will probably discover that as you do these projects, new ideas for experiments will come to mind—experiments that could make excellent science fair projects, particularly because the ideas are your own and are interesting to you.

If you decide to enter a science fair and have never done so before, you should read some of the books listed in the bibliography. The references that deal specifically with science fairs will provide plenty of helpful hints and lots of useful information that will enable you to avoid the pitfalls that sometimes plague first-time entrants. You will learn how to prepare appealing reports that include charts and graphs, how to set up and display your work, how to present your project, and how to relate to judges and visitors.

Safety First

Most of the projects included in this book are perfectly safe. However, the following safety rules are well worth reading before you start any project.

1. Do any experiments or projects, whether from this book or of your own design, under the supervision of a science teacher or other knowledgeable adult.

2. Read all instructions carefully before proceeding with a project. If you have questions, check with your supervisor before going any further.

3. Maintain a serious attitude while conducting experiments. Fooling around can be dangerous to you and to others.

4. Wear approved safety goggles when you are working with a flame or doing anything that might cause injury to your eyes.

5. Do not eat or drink while experimenting.

6. Have a first aid kit nearby while you are experimenting.

7. Do not put your fingers or any object other than properly designed electrical connectors into electrical outlets.

8. Never experiment with household electricity except under the supervision of a knowledgeable adult.

9. Do not touch a lit light bulb. Light bulbs produce light, but they also produce heat.

10. Many substances are poisonous. Do not taste materials you are using in experiments.

11. Keep flammable materials, such as alcohol, away from flames and other sources of heat.

12. If a thermometer breaks, inform your adult supervisor. Do not touch the broken glass with your bare hands. Always use an alcohol thermometer, never a mercury thermometer.

1

Matter: It Has Properties of Its Own

Matter is found in all kinds of shapes and in three different states—solid, liquid, and gas. Water, which is most commonly seen as a liquid, can easily be changed to a solid. Just put it in a freezer. If heated to boiling, water changes to a gas called steam. But it is still water. If the steam is cooled, the gas becomes liquid water again.

Although water is a liquid at room temperature, many other kinds of matter are not. Wood, for example, is a solid, while air is a gas. It is easy to forget that air is matter. However, when the wind blows or when you ride your bike very fast, you can feel the air pushing on you. During investigation 1.1, you will find that air is really matter. It can be weighed on a balance, and it takes up space. This is true of all other gases too.

1.1 Air Takes Up Space and Has Weight*

Fill a measuring cup or graduated cylinder about halfway with water. Note the water level. What is the volume of water in the measuring vessel? Add a few marbles or pebbles to the water. What happens to the water level? As you can see, the solids displace the water (push it out of the way). In fact, you can find the volume of the marbles by measuring how much water they displace. You simply measure the change in the water level.

The volume of many gases can also be determined by displacement of a liquid. However, gases ascend in liquids. They do not sink like marbles or stones. Therefore, the liquid is displaced downward rather than upward. To see this for yourself, turn a glass or a plastic cup upside down. Lower the glass or cup into a water-filled sink, pail, or large container as shown in Figure 1-1. Does water fill the glass? If you push the glass deeper, does water fill the space inside the inverted glass? What is in the glass that prevents water from entering?

Now *slowly* turn the glass until it is sideways. What happens to the air that was inside the glass?

With a friend to help, you can capture the air bubbles that escape from the glass. Repeat the experiment, but this time turn the air-filled glass sideways beneath another upside down water-filled glass. (See

Things you'll need:

- graduated cylinder or measuring cup
- water
- marbles or pebbles
- drinking glass or plastic cup
- deep sink, pail, or large container
- flexible drinking straw or a length of rubber or plastic tubing
- basketball, football, or soccer ball
- air pump
- needle valve used to empty and pump air into a ball
- platform balance that will measure changes of 0.1 g
- set of standard weights for balance

Figure 1-2.) Where do the bubbles go this time? What happens to the water in the upside down glass when the air bubbles enter the glass?

Hold a glass under water. Turn it until it is filled with water. Then turn it upside down under the water. Slowly lift the glass until its open end is just below the surface of the water. You will see that the pressure of the air can hold the water in the glass well above the water level in the sink, pail, or container. In fact, at sea level, the air will support a column of water that is 10 m (33 ft) tall.

If you have a flexible drinking straw, or a length of rubber or

Figure 1-1) Will water fill an upside down glass when it is pushed beneath the surface?

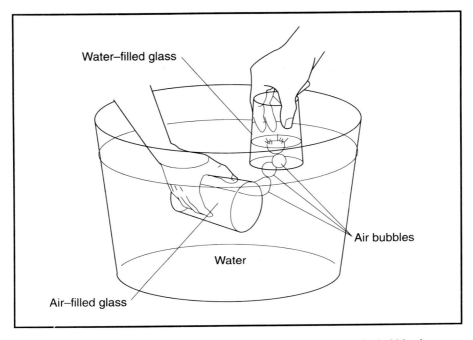

Water–filled glass

Air bubbles

Water

Air–filled glass

Figure 1-2) Pour the air upward from an air-filled glass. Capture the bubbles in a water-filled glass.

plastic tubing, how can you replace the water inside the upside down glass with your own "lung air"?

To see if air has weight, you will need a football, basketball, or soccer ball. Place a needle valve in the ball and let all the air out. Air will come out of the ball until the pressure of the air inside the ball is the same as the air pressure on the outside. Once air stops coming out of the ball, remove the needle valve and place the "empty" ball on a platform balance. How much does the ball weigh?

Now use the valve and an air pump to fill the ball with air until it is firm and ready for play. Again, remove the needle valve and weigh the ball. What does the ball weigh now? Does air have weight?

Air has much in common with other gases, but it is all around us and does not cost anything. In principle, you could do the same experiment with any gas. They all take up space and have weight.

Exploring on Your Own

- In experiment 1.1 you found that a ball weighs more after air is pumped into it. Will a plastic bag weigh more when filled with air? To find out, weigh a large, empty plastic bag. Then pull the bag through the air to fill it, and weigh it again. Has the weight changed? Why can you not weigh air this way?

- Weigh a large empty balloon. Fill the balloon with air and weigh it again. Why can you detect an increase in weight when a balloon is filled with air but not when a plastic bag is filled with air?

- What do you find when you try to weigh a helium-filled balloon? How can you explain this? Hint: think about what happens when you push a beach ball under the water and then release it.

- Place a balloon inside a bottle. Leave the mouth of the balloon outside the bottle as shown in Figure 1-3a. You will find it is impossible

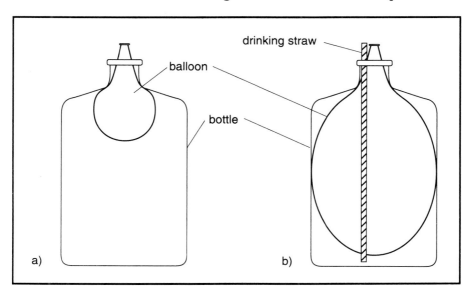

Figure 1-3a) Blowing up a balloon in a bottle: It is impossible to blow up a balloon that is inside a bottle. 1-3b) If a drinking straw is placed through the neck of the bottle, it becomes quite easy to blow up the balloon.

to blow up the balloon. Now place a drinking straw through the neck of the bottle as shown in Figure 1-3b. With the straw in place, you will find you can inflate the balloon quite easily. Why could you inflate the balloon when you used the straw?

Just for Fun

- See if you can use string and paper clips to make a helium balloon float, neither rising nor sinking, in the middle of a room.

Freezing and Boiling Points

In another book in this series (*Science Projects About Temperature and Heat*) you will find experiments that show that if water is cooled, it freezes at 0°C (32°F). If ice is warmed, it melts at the same temperature (0° C). This temperature is called the melting or freezing point of water.

If water is heated, its temperature rises until reaches 100°C (212°F). At that point, it boils (changes to a gas). The change from liquid to gas is evident from the bubbles of gas that form as the water boils. If hot steam is cooled, it condenses (changes to a liquid) at 100°C. Thus, the boiling point (and the condensing point) of water is 100°C.

As you can see from Table 1, the freezing and boiling points of different substances can be used to help identify them. Very few substances have the same freezing and boiling points.

Which of the substances in Table 1 are liquids at room temperature (20°C)? Which are solids? Which are gases? Would moth flakes melt if placed in boiling water?

Heaviness or Density

A gallon of milk weighs more than a quart, and a rock weighs more than a pebble. But does a baseball weigh the same as a tennis ball? Both are about the same size!

Lead is more than four times heavier than a piece of aluminum

TABLE 1: MELTING AND BOILING POINTS FOR A NUMBER OF SUBSTANCES.

Substance	Melting point (°C)	* Boiling point (°C)
Helium	-271	-269
Hydrogen	-259	-253
Oxygen	-219	-183
Nitrogen	-210	-196
Grain alcohol	-117	79
Wood alcohol	-98	65
Mercury	-39	357
Water	0	100
Napthalene (moth flakes)	79	218
Lead	327	1,525
Sodium chloride (salt)	801	1,413
Gold	1,063	2,660
Iron	1,530	3,000

*To convert celsius temperatures to Fahrenheit temperatures, multiply by 9/5 and then add 32.

that has the same volume. Lead is more *compact* or more "pushed together" than aluminum. A chemist would say that lead is more *dense* than aluminum.

The density of any piece of matter is the weight of the piece divided by its volume (the amount of space it takes up). A liter (L) of water, which is the same volume as 1,000 milliliters (mL) of water, weighs 1,000 grams (g) or 1 kilogram (kg). Therefore, the density of water is:

$$\frac{1000 \text{ g}}{1000 \text{ mL}} = 1.0 \text{ g/mL*} \quad \text{or} \quad \frac{1.0 \text{ kg}}{1.0 \text{ L}} = 1.0 \text{ kg/L}$$

*This can also be expressed as 1.0 g/cubic centimeter (g/cm^3) because a milliliter and a cubic centimeter are the same volume.

The fact that the density of water is 1.0 g/mL is not an accident.

Water was chosen to be the standard for measuring mass because it is so common. The weight of 1L of water at 4°C is defined as 1,000 g or 1.0 kg.

The densities of some common materials are found in Table 2. As you can see, very few things have the same density. Therefore, density is another property that is useful in identifying substances.

As you can see, gases have very low densities. Liquids are denser than gases, and solids are generally denser than liquids. (However, mercury is a liquid even though it is much denser than many solids.) Why do gases have such low densities? You will explore that question in project 1.2.

TABLE 2: THE DENSITIES OF SOME COMMON MATERIALS.

Substance	Density (g/cm^3)	Substance	Density (g/cm^3)
Hydrogen	0.000089	Water	1.00
Nitrogen	0.0013	Sea Water	1.03
Oxygen	0.0014	Glass	2.4-2.8
Carbon Dioxide	.0020	Aluminum	2.7
Wood (balsa)	0.11-0.13	Iron	7.9
Wood (oak)	0.60-0.90	Copper	8.9
Gasoline	0.69	Silver	10.5
Alcohol (wood)	0.7914	Lead	11.3
Alcohol (grain)	0.7893	Mercury	13.6
Olive Oil	0.92	Gold	19.3
Ice	0.92	Platinum	21.4

1.2 Density and Compressibility

Pull back the plunger piston of a syringe so that the cylinder is nearly filled with air. Place your finger tightly over the narrow, open end of the cylinder. Can you compress the gas by pushing the piston inward?

Things you'll need:

- plastic syringe (your school's science lab may have one you can use)
- water

Remove your finger and push the piston in as far as it will go. Place the open end of the syringe in water. Pull back on the piston so as to draw water into the cylinder. Again, seal the open end of the syringe with your finger. Can you compress the liquid?

What does this experiment tell you about the distances between gas molecules compared with the distances between liquid molecules?

Measuring the Densities of Some Substances

As you saw in project 1.2, the molecules of a gas must be far apart because a gas can be compressed into a much smaller volume. A liquid, on the other hand, is practically incompressible. This suggests that its molecules touch one another. The same is true of a solid.

If you can obtain a good balance (perhaps at your school), you can measure the density of a number of liquids and solids. The balance can be used to weigh a solid or a liquid. In the case of a liquid, you will have to subtract the weight of the container from the total weight to get the weight of the liquid. The volume of a liquid can be found by pouring the liquid into a graduated cylinder, medicine cup, or measuring cup. The volume of a solid can be found by measuring its dimensions or by finding out how much liquid it displaces. That is, you can measure out a volume of water, lower the solid into the water, and find the new volume of the water. The increase in volume must be due to the solid.

Can you show that the density of water is very close to 1.0 g/mL? What is the density of marbles, wood blocks, pieces of metal, rubbing alcohol, or cooking oil?

If you cannot find a good balance, you can still compare the densities of different materials by using a simple balance like the one you can build in project 1.3.

1.3 Comparing Densities*

Build a simple balance like the one shown in Figure 1-4. Use a rubber band to fasten the dowel or round pencil to the top of the ruler as shown. Be sure the dowel is fastened to the exact center of the ruler. Then use string to attach small paper or aluminum cup balance "pans" near each end of the ruler. The string can be held in place with tape. Be sure the cups are fastened near opposite ends of the ruler at exactly the same distance from the center of the ruler. The ends of the dowel can rest on two tin cans as shown. If the beam of your balance is not level, you can add a small piece of clay to the lighter side.

Once you have made your balance, you can use it to compare densities. You can do this by placing equal volumes of two different

Things you'll need:

- rubber band
- piece of dowel or round pencil
- one-foot (30-cm) ruler
- string
- small paper cups, such as soufflé cups or small aluminum cups
- tape
- two tin cans
- clay
- small wood block
- marble
- small stone
- steel washers
- rubbing alcohol
- cooking oil
- salt
- milk
- water

materials in the two pans of your balance. To begin, compare the weight of a small wood block with a clay block that you can mold into the same size and shape as the wood. Which block is more dense? Use the same method to compare the densities of marble and clay.

Which is more dense, a stone or steel washers? To find out, you can use a graduated cylinder or a medicine cup to obtain equal volumes of the two solids. (Remember, a solid displaces a volume of water equal to its own volume.) After drying the two equal volumes, place them on the balance pans. Which solid is more dense?

You can put equal volumes of different liquids in identical medicine cups or other small cups. Then you can use the balance to compare their densities. You might use water, rubbing alcohol, cooking oil, salt water, and milk. Which liquid is the most dense? Which liquid is the least dense? Do some of the liquids have densities that are nearly the same?

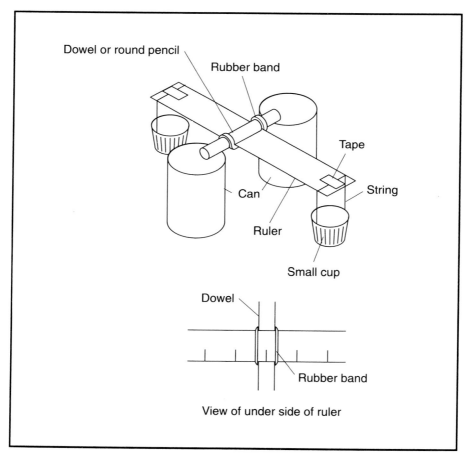

Figure 1-4) A balance that can be used to compare densities.

1.4 Comparing Densities with the Drop Method*

You probably found that the densities of water, salt water, and milk were not very different. In this investigation, you will find a way to compare the densities of liquids that have very nearly the same density. This method is based upon a principle that you probably know: less dense materials, such as wood, will float in more dense liquids, such as water.

You probably know from the last investigation that cooking oil is less dense than water. Based on that knowledge, what do you think will happen if you slowly and very gently squeeze a drop of cooking oil from an eyedropper into the center of a vial of water? (See Figure 1-5). Will the drop go up, down, or stay in the center? Try it! Were you right?

Things you'll need:

- four glasses (7-8 oz. capacity)
- alcohol
- food coloring (red, green, blue)
- salt
- cooking oil
- eyedropper
- four clear vials or medicine cups

What will happen if you squeeze a drop of alcohol into water or into cooking oil? What will happen if you squeeze a drop of water in cooking oil or into alcohol? You can make the water drops easier to see if you use a glass of water to which you have added a drop of two of food coloring.

To see how sensitive this test is, pour about 3/4 cup of water into each of four glasses. Add a tablespoonful of salt to one glass of water, two tablespoonsful to a second, and three tablespoonsful to a third. The fourth glass will contain only water. Stir the three glasses with salt until all the salt has dissolved (disappeared). Add two or three drops of different food colorings to the liquids. One could be colored red, another green, and a third blue. Leave the one without salt clear.

Pour samples of each liquid into four separate clear vials or medicine cups. Then, using an eyedropper, very carefully squeeze a drop of salt solution you colored red into the center of each of the other three samples of liquid. In which liquids does the red drop go up? In which liquids does it go down? Repeat the experiment using the salt solution you colored green. Which way does the green drop go in the other liquids? What are the results with drops of the other liquids?

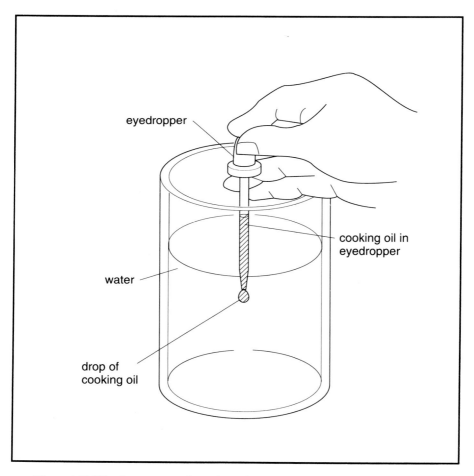

Figure 1-5) What happens to a drop of cooking oil when it is released in the middle of a water-filled container?

Based on your results, which is the densest liquid? Which is the least dense liquid? What is the density order (most dense to least dense) for these four liquids? You might like to add some other liquids to your density order. For instance, where would you place cooking oil in your density order? How about alcohol, vinegar, syrup, apple juice or other common liquids?

Exploring on Your Own

- If you change the shape of a piece of clay, will its weight change? Will its density change?

- Using the drop method, can you detect any difference in the densities of hot and cold tap water?

- How can you tell whether your bath soap is more or less dense than water?

- Half fill a tall jar with water. Put an uncooked egg in the jar. Does the egg sink or float? How does the density of the egg compare with the density of water? Next, prepare a salt solution by dissolving as much salt as possible in about 250 mL (0.5 pint) of water. Add a few drops of food coloring so that you can identify the salt solution from the plain water. Tip the jar and pour the salt solution slowly down the side of the jar. It will form a separate layer at the bottom of the jar. Where is the egg now? What can you conclude about the density of the egg?

Just for Fun

- Place a clear, transparent drinking straw in a glass of water. Wet your index finger and place it on the top opening of the straw as shown in Figure 1-6. If you keep your finger firmly over the opening, you will find that the water will stay in the straw when you lift it out of the glass. You have made a simple pipette. Once you have mastered the use of the pipette, see if you can use it to prepare

Figure 1-6) A drinking straw can be used as a pipette to pick up liquids.

two, three, and four layers of colored liquids in the straw. You can use the four liquids you prepared in project 1.4 to make the liquid layers. You might also use other colored liquids such as cooking oil, cranberry, apple and orange juices to increase the number of colored liquid layers.

Comparing the Densities of Gases

You know that gases have very low densities because their molecules are so far apart. Gases can be compressed to volumes that are only a thousandth as large as their normal volume. In fact, if you multiply the density of the gases found in Table 2 by 1,000, you will see that the numbers you get are close to the densities of liquids. During project 1.5, you will have a chance to compare the densities of gases.

1.5 Comparing Gas Densities

You can collect gases in balloons. Take two similar balloons and hang them from opposite ends of the ruler balance you used in investigation 1.2. (See Figure 1-7a). Tie bands can be used to hang the balloons from the beam. If one balloon seems to be a bit heavier than the other, add a small piece of clay to the tie band on the lighter balloon to make the beam level again.

Things you'll need:

- two balloons of the same size
- tie bands (twist-ties)

To compare the densities of air and carbon dioxide, you will need to make some carbon dioxide gas. To do this, break three or four seltzer tablets in half. Drop them into a small soda bottle that has about 3 cm (1 in) of water in the bottom. Immediately attach a balloon to the neck of the bottle. The balloon will swell as carbon dioxide gas is produced by the fizzing seltzer in the bottle. When the expansion of the balloon and the fizzing stops, seal off the neck of the balloon with a tie band. Fill the second balloon to the same size with air. You can use an air (tire) pump to add the air. Hang the two equal-sized balloons from opposite sides of the balance as before (Figure 1-7b). Which gas is denser?

Now replace the gas in the air-filled balloon with your "lung air." How does the density of lung air compare with that of carbon dioxide? How does it compare with that of air?

Expansion and Contraction

Another property of matter is the way it expands and contracts as its temperature changes. If you have read *Science Projects About Temperature and Heat*, you know how different substances expand and contract when heated or cooled. From the graphs in Figure 1-8, you can see that some liquids expand more than others when warmed through the equal changes in temperature. The same is true of solids

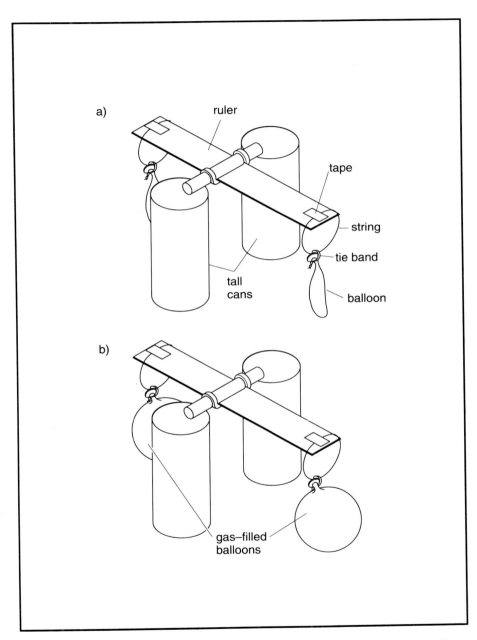

Figure 1-7) You can compare the densities of two gases by hanging equal-sized balloons filled with the two gases from opposite sides of a balance.

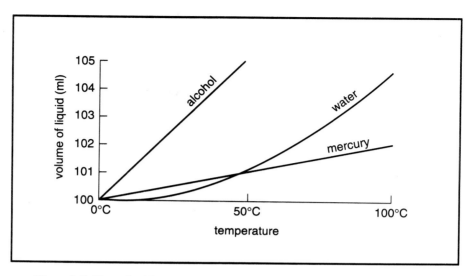

Figure 1-8) These liquids expand by different amounts when heated through equal tempererature changes.

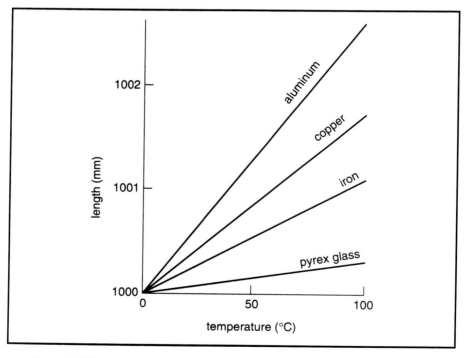

Figure 1-9) These four solids do not expand equally when warmed through the same change in temperature.

(Figure 1-9). As a result, the amount that a substance expands or contracts when heated or cooled can be used to help identify liquids and solids. On the other hand, all gases expand and contract with temperature in the same way. For each degree celsius increase in temperature, all gases expand by 1/273 of their volume. As a result, gases cannot be identified by their expansion or contraction when heated or cooled.

1.6 The Change in Volume When Water Freezes*

In a few minutes time, you can see what happens to the volume when water changes to ice. Fill a drinking glass with water. Place a transparent plastic drinking straw in the water. Let as much water as possible rise up into the straw. Then place your finger over the top of the straw as shown in Figure 1-10a. By keeping your finger pressed firmly

Things you'll need:

- drinking glass
- water
- transparent drinking straw
- clay or plasticine
- small container such as a baby food jar
- freezer

over the top opening in the straw, you can remove the straw and the water will stay in it. Air pressure will hold the water in the straw.

Press the bottom of the straw into a small lump of clay or plasticine on the bottom of a small jar as shown in Figure 1-10b. Now you can remove your finger. The clay will keep the water in the straw.

After you are sure the straw is not leaking, use a marking pen to mark the water level in the straw. Then place the jar in a freezer for about 20-30 minutes. After that time, check the straw. Has the water frozen? Has the volume changed? What happens to the volume of water as it changes to ice?

Law of Conservation of Mass

About 200 years ago, Benjamin Thompson (Count Rumford) did a similar experiment. But Thompson knew that water, unlike most substances, expands when it freezes. What he wanted to know was whether the weight of the water changes when it freezes. He found that there was no change in weight. Other experimenters have confirmed his finding. In fact, in a great variety of experiments, no one has ever found any change in mass* when substances undergo ordinary changes. Whether they melt, freeze, boil, decompose, or combine with other substances to form new compounds, the total mass of the materials does not change. These experimental results are summarized in the law of conservation of mass, which says that mass does not change.

*(The mass of something—the amount of matter in it—never changes. Its weight, which is the pull exerted on it by gravity, may change. For example, the weight of a stone would be less on the Moon where there is less gravity, but its mass would not change.)

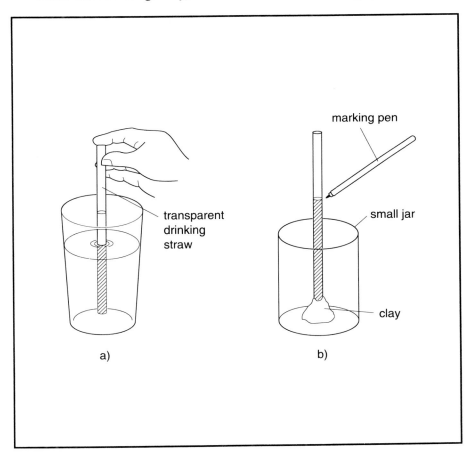

Figure 1-10) An experiment to find out what happens to the volume of water when it freezes.

Exploring on Your Own

- In experiment 1.6, you found that the volume increased when water changed to ice. Now you know that its mass did not change. What does this tell you about the density of ice compared with the density of water? How can you check your conclusion experimentally?

Just for Fun

- You can prepare some Gooey Green Glop by mixing in a bowl 1/2 cup of cornstarch with 1/4 cup of water and a few drops of green food coloring. Mix the liquids and solid with your hands. When you are finished, you will have difficulty deciding whether you have a solid or a liquid. Notice how Gooey Green Glop slides through your hands. See if it will flow through a hole in a piece of paper. If you would like to save Gooey Green Glop, put it in a covered container. If it has dried out when you want to use it again, add a few drops of water and it will be as strange as ever.

In the next chapter, you will not make anything as strange as Gooey Green Glop, but you will mix a number of different substances together. Many chemists, like cooks, spend a good part of their lives mixing things, not to prepare them for the oven, but to investigate questions about the nature of matter.

2

Solutions: Making Things Disappear

Have you ever wondered what happens to those flavored crystals that you stir into water to make a cool drink? Have you ever watched a spoonful of sugar disappear in a cup of hot tea? Even if you do not stir, the sugar crystals still disappear. When a solid disappears in a liquid, the solid is said to *dissolve* in the liquid. Chemists say that the *solute* (the solid material) dissolves in the *solvent* (liquid) to form a *solution*.

If molecules of water (the solvent) are actually touching one another, how can sugar crystals (the solute) fit in between them? Maybe there is some space between the molecules of water. Or maybe the sugar crystals push them apart and take up positions between them. The next investigation will help you to decide if there are any spaces between the molecules of liquids and between the particles of a grainy solid.

2.1 Does 1 + 1 Always Equal 2?*

If you do this experiment at school, you may be able to use two graduated cylinders. At home, you will probably have to use two measuring cups.

Half fill one graduated cylinder or measuring cup with water. Water and some other liquids are attracted to glass or plastic. As a result, the edges of the water that are touching the container are a little higher than the rest of the water

Things you'll need:

- two graduated cylinders (100 mL) or measuring cups
- fine dry sand
- water
- marbles
- clear jar
- rubbing alcohol
- eyedropper

(See Figure 2-1.) The lower line that you see at the surface is where most of the water is. It is called the meniscus. Be sure the bottom of the meniscus is right on the line that marks half the total volume of the graduated cylinder or measuring cup. If it is not, add or remove water with an eyedropper.

Half fill the other container with fine, dry sand. Then pour the sand slowly into the water. What is the total volume of the sand and water together? Why do you think the total volume is less than doubled? Could there be air spaces between the grains of sand?

You can use marbles to represent large or magnified grains of sand. If you put some marbles into a jar, can you see air spaces between the marbles? If there were air spaces between the grains of sand, what was the actual volume of the sand? Of the air?

Now, try adding one liquid to another to see if the volumes add as you might expect them to. Begin by half filling one graduated cylinder or measuring cup with water. Half fill the other measuring container with rubbing alcohol. Again, be sure the bottom of the meniscus is on the line that marks exactly half the volume. Now pour the alcohol into the water and stir. As you can see, the volume is slightly less than doubled (less than 100 mL or one cup). To see how much the volume has shrunk, use water and an eyedropper and count the number of drops of water you add to the container before the volume is exactly doubled. By how many drops did the volume "shrink" when the two liquids were mixed?

Do there seem to be spaces between the molecules of liquids?

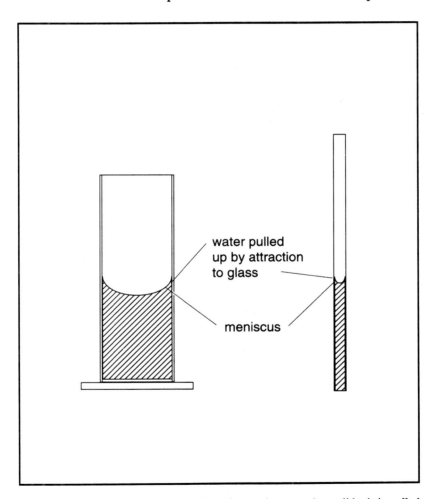

Figure 2-1) Because water is attracted to glass and many other solids, it is pulled upward where it touches the glass surface.

Exploring on Your Own

- Measure out half a cup of rice. Pour the rice into a jar. Then measure out half a cup of salt and pour it into the same jar. Cover the jar and shake it to mix the contents. Now pour the mixture of solids back into the measuring cup. Why is the volume less than 1 cup? If the rice represents molecules of water, what might the salt crystals represent?

Dissolving Solids in Water

From your experiment with sand and water, you know that not all solids dissolve in water. But for those solids that do, is there any limit to the amount that will dissolve? If there is, does it depend on the amount of water you use? Does it depend on the kind of solid you use? Does it depend on the temperature of the water? Will one dissolved solid interfere with the dissolving of another? Will solids dissolve in liquids other than water? In the next investigation, you will have a chance to explore some of these questions.

2.2 Solutions*

Pour 50 mL (1.7 oz) of water into each of two drinking glasses or beakers. Add a *level* teaspoonful of table salt (sodium chloride) to the water in one glass. You can use a file card to sweep off any salt above the edges of the spoon. Stir the water with another spoon for two minutes or until all the salt disappears.

To find out how much table salt the water will hold, stir in additional teaspoonfuls until no more will dissolve. Stir each teaspoonful you add for two minutes. If some

Things you'll need:

- measuring cup or graduated cylinder
- drinking glasses or beakers
- cold tap water
- two teaspoons
- file card
- table salt (Use kosher salt, if possible. Most commercial salt contains additives that make the solution cloudy.)
- Epsom salt

salt is left over after two minutes of stirring, stir for another minute to see if it will dissolve. If it does not, estimate what fraction of a teaspoonful remains and subtract it from the total you have added to the water. How many teaspoonfuls were you able to dissolve?

A liquid that holds as much solid as can possibly be dissolved is said to be *saturated*. How many teaspoonfuls of table salt did it take to make this saturated solution? Pour off the solution into another glass leaving behind any undissolved salt. Set this saturated solution aside. You will return to it shortly.

To the second glass or beaker of water, add a level teaspoonful of Epsom salt (magnesium sulfate) and stir as before. How many teaspoonfuls of Epsom salt are needed to make a saturated solution?

When you have dissolved all the Epsom salt that the water will hold, pour the solution you have made into another glass. Leave any undissolved salt in the first glass. Do you think any table salt will dissolve in this saturated solution of Epsom salt and water? Try it! Did it dissolve?

Do you think Epsom salt will dissolve in the saturated table salt solution that you prepared earlier? Test your prediction. Were you right?

Exploring on Your Own

- If you use twice as much water (100 mL or 3.3 oz), how much table salt do you think will dissolve? Test your prediction. Were you right? Can you predict the amount of table salt that will dissolve in 25 mL of water? Since temperature might affect the solubility of these solids, how should the temperature of the two different volumes of water compare?

- How does the amount of surface area a solid (solute) has affect the rate at which it dissolves? To find out, you will need a lump (or cube) of sugar and some loose (granulated) sugar. A sugar cube has the same volume as a teaspoonful of loose sugar, but less surface area is exposed because most of the sugar is inside the cube. Pour a level teaspoonful of sugar into 100 mL (3.3 oz) of water. Drop a cube of sugar into the same volume of water in a separate container. Watch carefully. In which container does the sugar dissolve faster? What do you conclude about the effect of surface area on the rate at which the sugar dissolves?

- What effect does stirring have on the dissolving process? To find out, add a teaspoonful of sugar to each of two glasses filled with warm water. Stir one, but not the other. In which glass does the sugar dissolve faster? Will the sugar eventually dissolve in both glasses?

- Does a level teaspoonful of table salt weigh the same as an equal volume of Epsom salt? How could you modify the experiments you have been doing so that you could compare the *weights* of table salt and Epsom salt that dissolve in 100 mL of water?

- You know that water freezes at 0°C (32°F). At what temperature will a saturated salt solution freeze? To find out, pour a saturated solution of table salt into a small jar. Put a thermometer in the liquid. Be sure the thermometer bulb is below the surface of the solution. Place the jar and thermometer in a freezer. Look at the thermometer every few minutes. Does the liquid freeze at 0°C the way water does? If not, at what temperature does the salt solution freeze? At what temperature do you think a saturated solution of Epsom salt will freeze?

2.3 Does Temperature Affect Solubility?*

The solubility of a solid is the amount of the substance that will dissolve in a certain volume of water. In project 2.2, you measured the solubility of table salt and Epsom salt, in terms of teaspoonfuls per 50 mL (1.7 oz) of water. In this experiment, you will test to see whether temperature affects their solubilities.

Things you'll need:

- same materials that were used in project 2.2
- alcohol thermometer
- hot tap water

Add 50 mL (1.7 oz) of *hot* tap water to a glass or beaker. Place the glass or beaker in a large pan of hot tap water so that the temperature will not change as you stir the solution. How many *level* teaspoonfuls of table salt will dissolve in the hot water? Be sure to stir thoroughly before you decide that the solution is saturated. How is the solubility of table salt affected by the temperature of the water?

Now repeat the experiment to see how temperature affects the solubility of Epsom salt in water. How do Epsom salt and table salt compare in terms of the effect of temperature on their solubilities?

Exploring on Your Own

- Your school science supplies may include potassium nitrate, which is a white, crystalline solid. If it does, ask your science teacher if you may use some for an experiment. Add 10 g of the solid to 10 mL of water in a test tube. Stir the mixture with a glass stirring rod until the solution is saturated. Then place the test tube in a Pyrex beaker half filled with warm water. Add some boiling chips or small pieces of limestone to the water in the beaker. This will prevent the water from "bumping" when you heat it to boiling **under adult supervision and while wearing safety glasses.** As you heat the beaker on a hot plate or stove, gently stir the undissolved solid and water. Can you get all the potassium nitrate to dissolve? Turn off

42

the heat and carefully remove the test tube and its contents from the hot water with a test tube holder. Place the test tube in a beaker of cold water. What happens as the solution cools to room temperature? Can you explain why this happens?

- Do you think a bouillon cube will dissolve faster in hot water or in cold water? Test your prediction.

2.4 Soluble and Insoluble Solids*

You have seen that both table salt and Epsom salt are soluble in water. However, their solubilities are not the same, and temperature does not affect their solubilities in the same way. In this experiment, you will test a number of other solids to see if they are soluble.

Try dissolving each of the solids listed under materials needed in 50 mL (1.7 oz) of cold tap water. Use just small amounts of the solids, say 1/8 teaspoonful. Which substances dissolve in water? Which do not? The ones that do not dissolve (the ones that continue to settle out after extensive stirring) are said to be insoluble. Which of the substances you tried are insoluble in water? Are any of the insoluble substances soluble in hot water?

Things you'll need:

- measuring cup or graduated cylinder
- drinking glasses or beakers
- cold tap water
- two teaspoons
- file card
- baking soda
- flour
- tooth powder
- starch
- instant coffee or tea
- Kool-Aid or other crystals used to make cold drinks

2.5 Other Liquids as Solvents

Liquids other than water are sometimes used to dissolve substances. Alcohol, for example, is often a solvent for things that will not dissolve in water.

You can try dissolving small amounts—1/10 teaspoonful—of solids (solutes) such as sugar, salt, baking soda, flour, tooth powder, starch, instant coffee or tea, and Kool-Aid or other crystals used to make cold drinks in various liquids. For liquids (solvents), you might try rubbing alcohol, soapy water (which you can make from liquid detergent and water), cooking oil, and vinegar. Which of the solids are soluble in alcohol? Which are soluble in soapy water? Which are soluble in cooking oil? Which are soluble in vinegar? What happens when you add baking soda to vinegar? Which of the solids are insoluble in the various liquids?

Things you'll need:

- same materials used in investigation 2.4
- salt
- sugar
- rubbing alcohol
- liquid detergent
- cooking oil
- white vinegar

2.6 Liquids in Liquids

You know from experiment 2.1 that alcohol and water are soluble in one another. Liquids that dissolve in one another this way are said to be *miscible*. Liquids that will not dissolve in one another are said to be *immiscible*.

Things you'll need:
- water
- cooking oil
- liquid detergent
- drinking glasses, test tubes, or beakers

Half fill a glass, beaker or test tube with tap water. Then pour a few drops of cooking oil into the water. Does cooking oil appear to be soluble in water? Try stirring or shaking the two liquids. Do they become miscible? Or do they separate again when you stop stirring? From your observations, how can you tell that cooking oil is less dense than water?

Add a few drops of liquid detergent to the mixture and stir again. Does the detergent have any effect on the rate at which the oil droplets separate from the water? Why are detergents used to wash clothes?

Will cooking oil dissolve in alcohol?

Exploring on Your Own

- Pour about 50 mL (1.7 oz) of alcohol into a glass or beaker that contains cooking oil. How can you tell that the liquids are not miscible? Use a drinking straw, pipette, or eyedropper to place a layer of water on the bottom of the glass. Once you have succeeded, how many distinct liquid layers can you see? How do the densities of water, cooking oil, and alcohol compare?

Just for Fun

- Prepare liquid layers of colored water (use food coloring), cooking oil, and alcohol in a jar that has a tight-fitting cap. Shake the mixture and watch the liquids settle and separate. Or turn the jar upside down and see what happens.

2.7 Gases Dissolved in Liquids

Look closely at what happens inside the bottle when you open a bottle of cold soda. How can you tell that gas was dissolved in the liquid? What do your observations tell you about the effect of reduced pressure on the solubility of a gas in a liquid?

Things you'll need:
- bottle of cold carbonated soda
- bottle of warm carbonated soda
- pan
- warm water

Now open another bottle of the same soda, but this time be sure the soda is *warm*. What do your observations tell you about the effect of temperature on the solubility of a gas in a liquid?

There is always some air (nitrogen and oxygen gases) dissolved in water. From your observations with the cold and warm soda, what do you expect to see if you place a glass of very cold water in a pan of warm water? Do an experiment to test your prediction. Were you right? Do you see any air bubbles forming as the water warms?

Gases Dissolved in Gases

Because most of the space occupied by a gas is empty, any gas will dissolve in any other gas. Air is a solution of primarily two gases—nitrogen (78 percent) and oxygen (21 percent). There are also small amounts of argon, carbon dioxide, water vapor (gas), and trace quantities of other gases. The solubility of water vapor in air increases with temperature. You may have noticed a cold pitcher of iced tea "sweating" on a hot summer day. The warm air has dissolved a lot of water, but the air in contact with the iced tea is cold. The water is less soluble in cold air and so it comes out of solution, condensing on the cold pitcher.

It is easy enough to mix things together, as any owner of a messy room can tell you. But it is not as easy to separate things once they are all mixed up. In Chapter 3, you will see that there are ways to separate mixtures. You will also see that solubility, as well as other properties, can be used to identify substances even when they are mixed with a number of other things that all look the same.

3

Analysis: Separating and Identifying Substances

When you dissolve salt in water, the solid seems to disappear into the liquid. Is there any way to separate the invisible, dissolved solid from the liquid? If you have a mixture of different substances, how can you separate them? Substances that look alike are not always the same substance. Is there some way to distinguish one substance from another? You already know that different substances have different properties such as solubility, odor, taste, density, melting point, boiling point, etc. In this chapter, you will learn how to separate mixtures and how to identify substances on the basis of their properties.

Separating Substances

If you mix salt and pepper, you can tell that it is a mixture. You can see that it is made up of distinct black and white particles. In fact, if time were no object, you could separate the particles with tweezers. On the other hand, if you look at a solution of salt and water, you cannot tell by looking whether you have pure water or a mixture of salt and water. In the next two investigations you will try to separate these very different kinds of mixtures.

3.1 Separating Things That Sink and Float*

In a bowl or a large jar, mix together either some sand and sawdust or some sand and powdered sulfur. It would be very difficult to pick out the individual particles of sand from the particles of sawdust or sulfur, even though you can see that they are different.

Add some water to the mixture. How does the water make it easy to separate the sand from the other particles?

Things you'll need:

- bowl or large jar
- sand
- sawdust or powdered sulfur
- water
- salt
- pepper

Separating Things that Dissolve and Do Not Dissolve

Mix together some sand and salt. Can you distinguish between salt and sand particles in the mixture? How can you use water to separate the salt from the sand?

Separating Salt and Pepper

Now that you have had some experience separating substances, prepare a mixture of salt and pepper. Then design your own method for separating the components of the mixture.

Exploring on Your Own

- Your school's science supplies may include some iron filings and a magnet. If they do, ask your science teacher if you may use them.

Bring the magnet near a small pile of iron filings. What happens? How can you use the magnet to separate a mixture of sand and iron filings? Can you use the same method to separate a mixture of salt and iron filings, a mixture of sugar and iron filings, or a mixture of small steel and brass washers?

3.2 Separating a Dissolved Solid from Its Solvent*

Prepare a solution by dissolving some salt in water. Remove several drops of the solution with an eyedropper and place them on a glass plate or on a piece of plastic wrap. Leave the drops for several hours. What is left after the water evaporates?

You can see this effect on a larger scale and with different solids. You can buy table salt and Epsom salt in a store. Your science teacher may be able to supply you with alum and copper sulfate. Prepare saturated solutions of as many of these solids as possible. You can do this by dissolving each solid in a small container or test tube that contains about 30 mL (1 oz) of water.

Things you'll need:

- salt (preferably kosher salt)
- water
- small containers, such as baby food or jelly jars, or test tubes
- eyedropper
- glass plate or plastic wrap
- saucers
- Epsom salt
- alum
- copper sulfate
- pencil and paper or marking pen
- magnifying glass

After you have prepared the solutions, pour them onto separate saucers. Label each saucer so that you know which dissolved solid is in each one. If possible, place the saucers in a warm place. Examine the solutions periodically as the water evaporates. Once the water has evaporated, examine the crystals that remain with a magnifying glass. Describe the shape and color of the crystals that form on each saucer. Could you use the crystals that form as the water evaporates to identify the solids you dissolved? Ask your teacher or adult supervisor to tell you how to dispose of the copper sulfate crystals.

Exploring on Your Own

- Often chemists do not want to wait for water to evaporate. They speed up the process by boiling the solution. Figure 3-1 shows a set up that can be used to separate dissolved salt from water. The water boils away, condenses in the tubing, and is collected in a container at the end of the tubing. Perhaps your science teacher will help you set up the apparatus shown in Figure 3-1. **In any event, do not attempt to insert the bent glass tube into the rubber stopper unless your teacher is present to help you. Be sure you wear safety glasses and have an adult to supervise you before you**

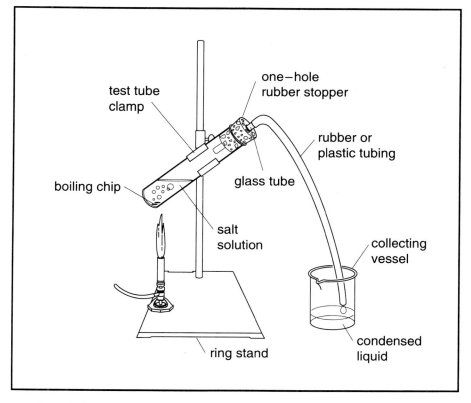

Figure 3-1) Separating salt from water by boiling the liquid and then condensing the gas in another place is called distillation.

heat the solution in the test tube. Be sure also to **place a boiling chip in the bottom of the test tube.** It will allow the solution to boil smoothly. Heat the test tube gently until the water boils. Then watch the condensed liquid fall from the end of the tubing. Place a drop of the condensed liquid on a glass plate and let it evaporate. Is there any salt in the condensed liquid? What is left in the vessel where boiling took place after all the water has boiled away? **Be sure to remove the heater just before all the water has boiled away!**

- Can this method be used to separate a solution made by dissolving a drop of ink in water? A drop or two of food coloring dissolved in water? **Before attempting to answer these questions, be sure you are wearing safety glasses and have an adult to supervise you.**

Just for Fun

- Prepare a saturated salt solution. Then use a water color brush to paint your name with the salt solution on a sheet of black construction paper. Set the paper aside to dry. The next day you will see your name in white crystals across the black background.

Identifying Some White Solids

Some chemists spend a good part of their time trying to identify unknown substances found in water supplies, at the scene of a crime, in the air, in chemical processes and so forth. Chemists who do this are called analytical chemists. At the end of the next investigation, you will be asked to identify one or more of five solids in a mixture. At the beginning of the investigation, you will learn to identify these substances by means of a number of tests. Some of these tests involve solubility, which you already know about. Others involve seeing what happens when the substances are heated or combined with certain chemicals.

3.3 Detecting Unknown Solids

Obtain about 1/4 cup of salt, sugar, flour, baking soda, and baking powder. Keep these white solids separated and in *labeled* paper cups. Be careful not to get them mixed up. You will carry out a number of tests on each solid to see how they behave in the presence of heat and other chemicals.

Test 1: Solubility and/or Reaction with Water

Line up five small jars. Place a small amount (about 1/4 teaspoonful) of salt in the first one, an equal amount of sugar in the second one, and so on until you have samples of all five solids in separate jars. If possible, have a separate plastic spoon or wooden coffee stirrer for each solid to be sure you do not mix them. Otherwise, wash and dry the spoon or stirrer after transferring each solid. Add about 50 mL (2 oz) of water to each jar. Stir the solids and water with wooden coffee stirrers or toothpicks. Which of the solids are soluble in water? Do any of the solids react with water to produce bubbles of gas?

Things you'll need:
- salt
- sugar
- flour
- baking soda
- baking powder
- paper cups
- plastic spoons or wooden coffee stirrers
- water
- small jars such as baby food jars (at least five)
- wooden coffee stirrers or flat toothpicks
- eyedropper
- tincture of iodine
- white vinegar
- small aluminum cups or pans
- wooden spring-type clothespin or forceps
- candle, Sterno, hot plate, or alcohol burner

Test 2: Vinegar

Again, place small samples of each solid in five separate small jars. Add about 20 mL (0.75 oz) of vinegar to each solid. Which of the solids react with vinegar to produce bubbles of gas?

Test 3: Iodine

Prepare a dilute solution of iodine by adding ten drops of tincture of iodine to about two hundred drops of water in a small jar. Save this solution. You will use it here and in later tests as well. Add a drop or two of the iodine solution to each of the solids in separate small jars. Which one or ones become dark blue in color when mixed with the iodine solution? **When the iodine solution is gone, wash the jar thoroughly with soap and water. Iodine is poisonous.** If any iodine solution is left over, you may want to save it to use in one of the *Exploring on Your Own* experiments that follow experiment 3.3.

Test 4: Heat

Because you will be using heat and possibly a flame in this test, work only under adult supervision. Be sure you wear safety glasses while heating the solids. Place small samples of each in small aluminum cups or pans. Use a wood spring-type clothespin or forceps to hold the pans, each in turn, over a flame or to place them on a hot plate. What happens to each solid as it is heated? Do any of them melt? Do any of them turn dark?

Identifying White Solids

Now that you have done a number of tests that help you to identify the various solids, see whether you can identify these solids when they are mixed together. Ask a friend, parent, or teacher to prepare a mixture of two or more of the white solids you have been working with. Then see if you can identify the solids that are in the mixture. **Remember: You are to wear safety goggles and have an adult to supervise you whenever you heat substances!**

If you enjoy the challenge of identifying all the solids that are in the mixture of the white powders, ask for additional and different mixtures. How good are you at identifying the solids in these other mixtures?

Exploring on Your Own

• Based on the tests you did during experiment 3.3, do you think baking powder might contain a mixture of white powders? If so, what white solids might you expect to find in baking powder? To check your prediction, read the list of ingredients on a can of the powder. Does the list include the substances you predicted were there?

• Place small samples of white bread, a white cracker, a piece of potato, a piece of apple, a piece of cheese, and a piece of white paper on a sheet of plastic wrap. Then add a drop of the iodine solution you prepared for investigation 3.3 (ten drops of tincture of iodine with two hundred drops of water) to each sample. Which samples contain starch? How do you know?

• Bite off a small piece of a white cracker or a piece of white bread. Chew the piece for about 5 minutes mixing it thoroughly with saliva. Then gently spit the mixture into a small glass jar. Add a drop of the iodine solution to the chewed cracker or bread. How does the color compare with the color you found when you tested the sample before? What evidence do you have that saliva contains a chemical that changes starch to something else? **Do not taste the cracker after adding the iodine. Remember that iodine is poisonous.**

Just for Fun

- Use the wide end of a toothpick as a "pen" to write an invisible message. Lemon juice will serve as your invisible "ink." Write the message on a small sheet of white paper. When the lemon juice has dried, dip the paper in a saucer that contains 1/8 cup of water to which you have added two drops of tincture of iodine. The paper will turn blue because it contains starch. But the citric acid in lemon juice combines with iodine to form a clear substance. Thus, your message will appear as light letters on a dark background, at least for a few seconds.

In the tests you used to identify the white solids, you saw starch turn a dark blue color when iodine was added to it. You saw bubbles of gas form when vinegar was added to baking soda. You may have seen sugar and flour darken when you heated them. All these changes that you saw were examples of chemical reactions. In Chapter 4, you will investigate a number of chemical reactions including a detailed investigation of the reaction between baking soda and vinegar.

4

Chemical Reactions: When New Substances Form

When two or more different substances combine and form a new substance—one that was not there before—we say a chemical reaction has occurred. For example, if two clear liquids are mixed together and a yellow solid appears, a chemical reaction has taken place. The yellow solid is a new substance that was not there before. If two substances are mixed together and bubbles appear, it indicates that a new substance, a gas, is being generated. You saw such a reaction in Chapter 3 when you added vinegar to baking soda. Similarly, the appearance of a solid, a new color (as when iodine is added to starch), or a rapid change in temperature when substances are mixed, all indicate that a chemical reaction is taking place.

Not all changes involve chemical reactions. For example, the melting of ice to form water is not a chemical change because no new substance is formed. Water is simply the melted form of ice. If you put the water in a freezer, it will change back to ice. On the other hand, pouring the yellow solid described in the previous paragraph back into water will not produce the two original clear solutions.

If you dissolve salt in water, there is no chemical reaction. The salt disappears but no new substance appears. You can get the salt back again by simply letting the water evaporate. However, you cannot get back baking soda and vinegar by mixing the gas produced when they react with the liquid that is left after the reaction.

The next few investigations will allow you to explore a familiar chemical reaction in some detail.

4.1 Some Chemical Reactions from the Kitchen*

Place about half a teaspoonful of baking soda in a glass. Add about 30 mL (1 oz) of vinegar to the baking soda. Is a gas produced; that is, do you see a lot of bubbles being generated? Is a chemical reaction taking place? How do you know?

Repeat the experiment, but this time add water to the baking soda instead of vinegar. Is there a chemical reaction between the baking soda and the water? Now stir the mixture of baking soda and water. Does the baking soda dissolve? Can you make it all dissolve? (Add more water if necessary.)

Things you'll need:

- teaspoon
- baking soda (sodium bicarbonate)
- clear container such as a drinking glass or plastic cup
- white vinegar
- water
- citric acid crystals or crystals used to make lemonade such as Kool-Aid
- seltzer tablets

Pour off about half of the solution. What do you think will happen if you add some vinegar to the baking soda solution? Try it! Were you right?

To a clean, dry glass add about half a teaspoonful of baking soda and an equal amount of citric acid or a teaspoonful of Kool-Aid crystals, which contain citric acid. Now add some water to the solids. What happens?

From what you have seen so far, what do you think would happen if you added some lemon juice to some dry baking soda in a container? Try it! Were you right?

Ask your science teacher to help you add a few milliliters of **dilute** hydrochloric acid to some baking soda in a glass beaker. **Be sure you both wear safety goggles when you do this.** Can you predict what will happen? Can you fill in the blank in the following chemical reaction with a general term (not a specific term such as vinegar or citric acid)?

sodium bicarbonate + _____ ⇒ gas + a sodium salt

Drop a seltzer tablet in a glass of water. What evidence do you have that a chemical reaction is taking place?

4.2 A Look at the Seltzer and Water Reaction*

You have seen that when a seltzer tablet is placed in water a chemical reaction occurs. You know this because a new substance (a gas) is produced. What causes the reaction? Is a seltzer tablet made of one substance, or is it a mixture? If you read the list of ingredients on the package, you will see that all seltzer tablets include aspirin, citric acid, and sodium bicarbonate (baking soda). Some brands also contain mono-calcium phosphate. Since not all seltzer tablets contain mono-calcium phosphate, it must not be essential for the reaction that produces the gas.

Things you'll need:

- seltzer tablets
- water
- teaspoon
- aspirin
- baking soda (sodium bicarbonate)
- citric acid or Kool-Aid crystals

By mixing different samples of the ingredients, you can find out which ones react in water to form the gas. In a dry glass, mix about half a teaspoonful of citric acid or Kool-Aid crystals with a crushed aspirin tablet. Add some water to the mixture. Is a gas produced? Next, add water to a dry mixture of aspirin and baking soda. Finally, test a dry mixture of baking soda and citric acid (or Kool-Aid crystals). Based on your tests, which ingredients in a seltzer tablet combine to form a gas when water is added? If more than one reaction takes place, which one produces the most gas?

Read once more the list of ingredients found in baking powder. Based on what you have learned in this experiment, explain why baking powder reacts with water to form a gas.

Exploring on Your Own

- A change in color indicates a chemical reaction because different

65

substances have different colors. Put on safety goggles to protect your eyes. Add a drop or two of black ink or food coloring to a few milliliters of water in a small jar. **Ask an adult to help you as you add a few drops of household bleach, which is poisonous,** to the colored solution. Stir the mixture and continue adding bleach until you have evidence of a chemical change. What is the evidence? What happens if you now add another drop of ink or food coloring to the solution? **Be sure to wash everything thoroughly after you finish this experiment.**

Just for Fun

• Place a one-liter (or one-quart) soda bottle in the center of a large pan. Then pack sand, gravel, or dirt around the bottle as shown in Figure 4-1. Add about two tablespoonsful of baking soda to the

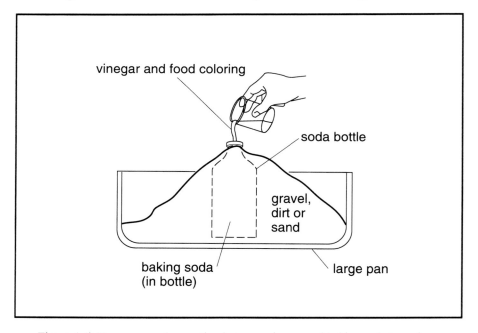

vinegar and food coloring

soda bottle

gravel, dirt or sand

baking soda (in bottle)

large pan

Figure 4-1) You can use the reaction between vinegar and baking soda to make a "volcano."

bottle. If you place the white solid on a folded piece of paper, it will be easier to pour it into the bottle. Next, add a few drops of red and yellow food coloring to a cup of white vinegar. Pour the vinegar into the bottle. Then stand back and watch the volcano erupt!

4.3 Changing the Speed of a Chemical Reaction*

You know now why seltzer tablets react when placed in water. The sodium bicarbonate (baking soda) and citric acid combine to form a gas that bubbles out of the solution. In addition, some sodium citrate (a type of salt) and water are produced, which remain in the solution.

Things you'll need:
- hot and cold water
- drinking glasses or clear plastic cups
- seltzer tablets
- clock or watch with second hand

Do you think temperature will affect the speed at which a seltzer tablet reacts with water? To find out, place equal amounts of hot and cold water in separate, clear, identical containers. Drop a seltzer tablet into each container of water. In which one does the reaction seem to go faster? You can use a watch or a clock with a second hand to compare the times for each tablet to dissolve completely. What do you conclude about the effect of temperature on the rate at which a seltzer tablet reacts with water? Why do you think food cooks faster in a hot oven than in a warm one?

To see if the amount of surface area affects the rate of a reaction, you will need two more seltzer tablets. Leave one tablet whole; crush the other one into tiny pieces so that the tablet will have more of its surface exposed. Now drop both tablets into equal volumes of water in two separate but identical containers. Why should the water temperature be the same in both containers? Which tablet reacts faster? How does the amount of surface area affect the rate of the reaction?

Will the amount of water into which you put a seltzer tablet affect the speed of the reaction? Design an experiment to find out.

Do you think the speed of the reaction will depend on the amount of seltzer used? To find out, drop a *whole* seltzer tablet into, say, half a cup of water. At the same time, drop *half* a tablet into an equal amount of water in an identical cup. In which container is gas produced faster? (Remember, if the reaction speed is the same in both containers, it will take the whole–tablet just twice as long to react as the half–tablet.) Based on your results, predict how long it will take one-quarter tablet to react with the same amount of water.

If you drop a seltzer tablet into a container of water where several tablets have already reacted, there will be a lot of the products of the reaction (some dissolved gas and the sodium citrate) in the solution. Do you think this will affect the speed of the reaction between the seltzer and water? Design an experiment to find out.

You can increase the concentration of one of the products of the reaction, namely, the gas, by placing the palm of your hand firmly over the top of the container where the reaction is taking place. This will prevent the gas from escaping and raise the gas pressure above the liquid. How does this increase in pressure affect the rate that bubbles form in the vessel? What happens to the rate of the reaction when you remove your hand?

Exploring on Your Own

- Will seltzer tablets react with liquids other than water? If they will, how do you think the speed of the reaction will compare with its rate of reaction in water? Place equal amounts of water, white vinegar, rubbing alcohol, salt water, carbonated soda, and a solution of baking soda (all at the same temperature) in identical containers. In which liquids do you think there will be a reaction when a seltzer tablet is added? How do you think the reaction speeds will compare in the different liquids?

- Bromo-Seltzer, which is made up of tiny pellets, contains sodium bicarbonate and citric acid too. Weigh out an amount of Bromo-Seltzer that has the same weight as a single seltzer tablet. Drop the two seltzer samples into equal amounts of water in identical clear containers. Which sample do you think will react faster? Were you right?

- Do you think it will make any difference if you put the two samples into dry containers and then pour in equal volumes of water? Test this prediction too!

4.4 Gas Volumes from the Seltzer and Water Reaction*

You can collect the gas that forms when seltzer tablets react with water by using the apparatus shown in Figure 4-2. Fill a large, wide-mouthed plastic or glass bottle with water and invert it in a pail of water. Then pour 20 mL (0.7 oz) of water into the flask. Break a seltzer tablet in half and add it to the flask. Quickly place the stopper in the neck of the flask and the end of the tubing under the mouth of the inverted jar. The bubbles of gas emerging from the tube will collect in the bottle displacing water from it.

Things you'll need:

- large, clear glass or plastic bottle
- plastic pail
- water
- graduated cylinder or measuring cup
- small flask or soda bottle
- seltzer tablets
- single-hole rubber stopper
- short length of glass tubing or flexible soda straw
- rubber or plastic tubing or flexible straws
- marking pen

Swirl the flask until no more gas bubbles rise in the bottle. Then remove the tube from the pail. Mark the water level in the bottle with a marking pen. Remove the bottle from the pail and fill it to the mark with water. You can measure the volume of the water in the bottle by pouring it into a graduated cylinder or measuring cup. What volume of gas was produced when one seltzer tablet was added to 20 mL of water?

Now try to predict how much gas will be produced if two seltzer tablets are added to 40 mL (1.3 oz) of water. Carry out the experiment to see if you are correct.

How much gas will be produced if half a seltzer tablet is added to 10 mL (0.3 oz) of water?

71

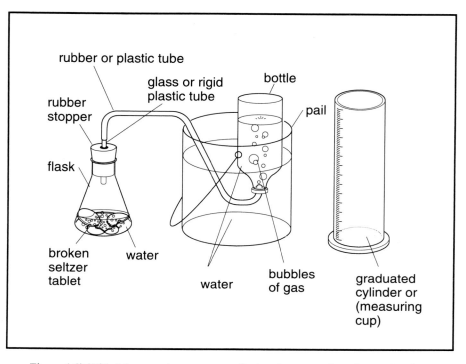

Figure 4-2) With this apparatus, you can collect and measure the volume of carbon dioxide produced when seltzer reacts with water.

Exploring on Your Own

- What happens to the volume of gas produced if you add two seltzer tablets to *20* mL of water instead of 40 mL as you did in project 4.4? Can you explain why the results are different this time?

- Will the volume of gas produced be different if you place the end of the rubber or plastic tube near the top of the inverted bottle rather than at the bottom? Can you explain why?

Just for Fun

- You can make a seltzer tablet fire extinguisher. Place a birthday candle at the center of a wide-mouth jar. Use a small piece of clay

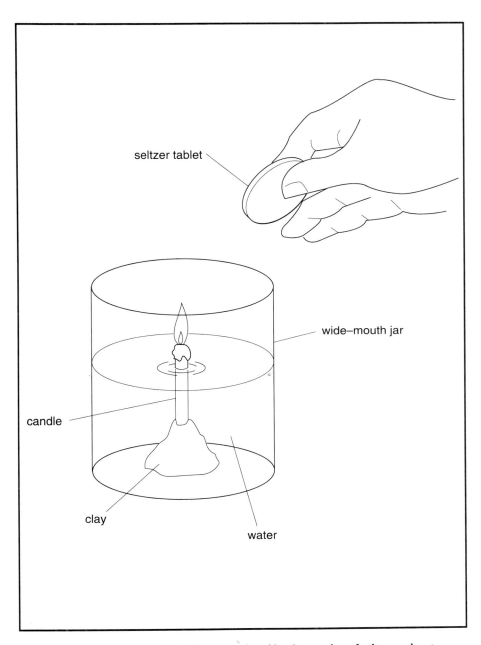

seltzer tablet

wide–mouth jar

candle

clay

water

Figure 4-3) Watch to see how the gas produced by the reaction of seltzer and water can put out a flame.

to support the candle as shown in Figure 4-3. Then carefully fill the jar about half-way by pouring water into one side of the jar. Be careful not to wet the candle wick.

Ask an adult to light the candle. Let the candle burn until the wick is near the water level in the jar. Then carefully drop a seltzer tablet into the water. You will see the candle flame go out as gas fills the jar above the water.

4.5 What Gas Is Produced When Seltzer Reacts with Water?

If you did the *Just for Fun* activity that precedes this investigation, you know that the gas produced by the reaction of seltzer with water will put out a flame. This suggests that the gas might be the same gas that is found in some fire extinguishers, namely, carbon dioxide.

In this investigation, you will use a balloon to collect the gas produced when seltzer reacts with water. This can be done by placing a balloon over a one–hole rubber stopper attached to one end of the glass or plastic tube as shown in Figure 4-4a. The one-hole rubber stopper at the other end of the tube should fit the neck of a small soda bottle or flask where the gas will be produced. Once you have collected the gas in the balloon, you can bubble it into limewater. Limewater is used to identify carbon dioxide. If the gas is carbon dioxide, it will turn the limewater milky.

If your school's science supplies include limewater, ask if you may use some. If not, you can prepare limewater by mixing lime (calcium oxide) and water in a bottle. Seal the bottle and shake the contents thoroughly to dissolve as much lime as possible. Then let any excess solid settle out overnight. Pour the liquid above the solid into another bottle and *seal* it shut.

Place about 25 mL (0.8 oz) of water in the bottom of a small soda bottle or flask. Break a seltzer tablet in half and drop it into the bottle. Quickly insert the stopper into the neck of the flask or bottle (Figure 4-4b). When the reaction is over and the balloon stops expanding, seal

Things you'll need:

- small flask or soda bottle
- water
- seltzer tablet
- two one-hole rubber stoppers, one should fit the mouth of the flask or bottle
- short length of glass or plastic tubing
- balloon
- limewater or lime
- two small bottles with tops

the neck of the balloon with your thumb and finger. Remove the glass or plastic tube from the lower stopper and place the end of it into about 20 mL of limewater in a small jar or beaker as shown in Figure 4-4c. Release the bubbles of gas slowly so that you can count bubbles. Does the limewater turn milky? If it does, how many bubbles of gas were required? Can you identify the gas produced by the reaction of seltzer with water?

You may have heard that you breathe out carbon dioxide from

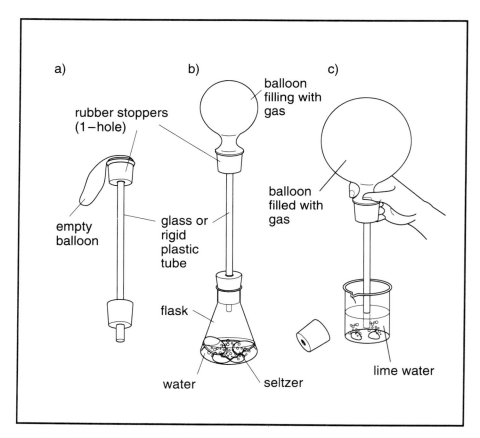

Figure 4-4) Collecting and testing the gas produced by the reaction of seltzer tablets and water. 4-4a) Apparatus to carry gas from flask to balloon. 4-4b) Gas produced in flask collects in balloon. 4-4c) Slowly release bubbles of gas into the limewater.

your lungs. To see if this is true, use a drinking straw to bubble some of the air you exhale into the same amount of limewater you used before. Again, count the bubbles. Does the limewater turn milky? If it does, how many bubbles were required this time? Does the air you exhale contain carbon dioxide? Based on the number of bubbles, how does the concentration (amount per bubble) of carbon dioxide in your breath compare with that in seltzer-water gas?

More Chemical Reactions

In the last five investigations you have looked closely at the reaction between seltzer tablets and water, a reaction that is primarily between sodium bicarbonate and citric acid. In that reaction, the new substance produced is a gas—carbon dioxide. Gases are produced in other chemical reactions too, but in some reactions a new solid or liquid is formed. In others, there is no visible change but a change in temperature or tests with indicators such as iodine may reveal that new substances have formed. During project 4.6 you will see reactions in which a gas is *not* formed. See if you can figure out what happens in each case to indicate that there is a chemical reaction.

4.6 Some Other Chemical Reactions

A Reaction Between Epsom Salt and Ammonia

Start this experiment in the morning because the reaction is slow. Add a teaspoonful of Epsom salt to about 40 mL (1.3 oz) of water in a small jar or beaker. Stir until the salt dissolves. Then pour about 20 mL (0.7 oz) of ammonia into the water. Do not stir! Leave the chemicals to react slowly as they mix. Notice that after a few minutes it begins to look as though a fog is forming inside the liquid.

Look at the chemicals periodically during the day to see what is happening. What evidence do you have that a chemical reaction has taken place? Is the white substance formed more or less dense than the liquid it is in? How do you know?

The white substance that has formed and settled is magnesium hydroxide. To see if you can separate this white solid from the liquid,

Things you'll need:

- teaspoon
- Epsom salt (magnesium sulfate)
- water
- small jar, such as baby food jar or beaker
- measuring cup or graduated cylinder or medicine cup
- clear household ammonia
- coffee filter or filter paper
- funnel
- tall glass or beaker
- white vinegar
- steel wool (no soap)
- toothpick
- paper towel
- saucer
- vinegar
- pennies

fold a coffee filter or a piece of filter paper as shown in Figure 4-5a. Put the cone–shaped filter you have made in a funnel (Figure 4-5b). Place the funnel on top of a tall glass or beaker. Then very gently pour the liquid and the finely divided white solid down a straw or glass rod onto the filter paper (Figure 4-5c). Allow the material to flow slowly

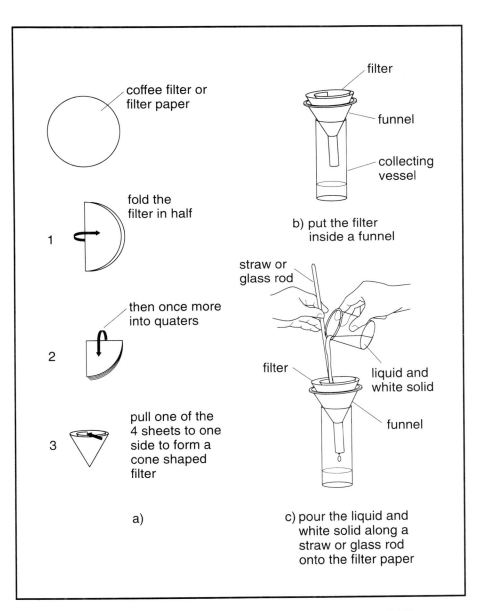

coffee filter or
filter paper

filter

funnel

collecting
vessel

fold the
filter in half

1

b) put the filter
inside a funnel

straw or
glass rod

then once more
into quaters

2

filter

liquid and
white solid

pull one of the
4 sheets to one
side to form a
cone shaped
filter

3

funnel

a)

c) pour the liquid and
white solid along a
straw or glass rod
onto the filter paper

Figure 4-5a) Making and using a filter: 1. Fold the filter in half. 2. Then fold it once more into quarters. 3. Pull one of the sheets to one side to form a cone-shaped filter. 4-5b) Put the filter inside a funnel. Put the funnel in a tall jar or beaker. 4-5c) Pour the liquid and white solid along a drinking straw or glass rod onto the filter paper.

through the filter. The filter has tiny pores in it. These pores allow small particles such as molecules of water and very small solid particles to pass through. Does the filter prevent all the white particles from flowing through it? How can you tell?

Remove the filter paper from the funnel. Open it up and put it on a paper towel. Leave it there until the white solid that has collected on it is dry. Then scrape the white solid into a small jar. Cover the jar and save it for use in Chapter 5.

A Reaction Between Iron and Vinegar and Ammonia

Cut a square about 2 cm (1 in) on a side from a steel wool pad (not a soaped pad). Place the steel wool in a jar and cover it with vinegar. Put the top securely on the jar and leave it for 4-5 days. The iron in the steel wool will react with the acetic acid in the vinegar to form soluble iron acetate.

After 4-5 days, pour about 20 mL (0.7 oz) of the solution into another jar or beaker. Add an equal volume of ammonia and stir. The green slime that forms is iron hydroxide (ferrous hydroxide).

Filter the iron hydroxide as you did the magnesium hydroxide in the previous experiment. Does any of the green slime come through the filter paper? What happens to the color of the green hydroxide on the filter paper? Use a toothpick to look beneath the outer layer of solid on the filter paper. What do you find underneath?

Use the toothpick to transfer a little of the solid on the filter paper to a small jar or beaker. You know that the material is not soluble in water. Is it soluble in vinegar? How can you find out? Is it soluble in ammonia?

A Reaction Between Pennies and Vinegar

Fold a white paper towel twice so it is one-quarter its original size. Pour some vinegar onto a saucer and place the paper towel on the saucer so it is wetted by the vinegar. Then place three or four pennies on the paper. Leave the setup overnight. On the next day examine the pennies closely. What evidence is there that a chemical reaction has taken place?

The green coating that you see on the pennies is copper acetate. The acetate part of the compound came from the vinegar. Where did the copper part of the compound come from?

Exploring on Your Own

- Can you separate ink or food coloring from water by pouring the mixture through a filter? To find out, fold a coffee filter or filter paper as described in Figure 4-5a. Place the filter in a funnel and pour a mixture of water and black ink or water and food coloring onto it. Is the liquid that comes through the filter paper clear or is it still colored? What happens to the color on the filter?

- You may have noticed that the color in the ink or food coloring on the filter in the previous experiment seemed to separate into colors that were not visible before. You can find out if different samples of ink and food coloring are mixtures of other colors by a process called *paper chromatography*. To do this, cut some strips about 2 cm x 15 cm (1 in x 6 in) from coffee filters or filter paper. Near the bottom of each strip paint a stripe with each of your colored samples. Use different colored marking pens to "paint" on the inks. Use a toothpick to paint on stripes of food coloring. After the colored stripes are dry, hang the paper strips as shown in Figure 4-6. The bottom ends of the strips should just touch the water in a wide container. What happens as the water climbs the paper? Do any of the colors separate into new colors? What ones do not? Are any of the colors insoluble in water? How do you know?

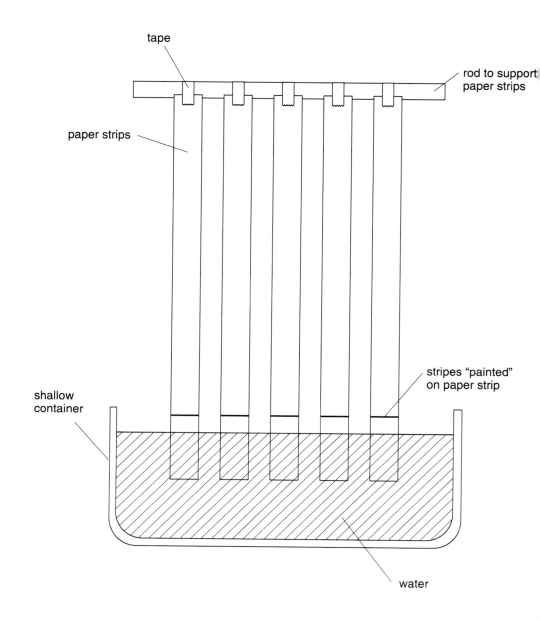

Figure 4-6) Paper chromatography can be used to separate the colors in ink and food coloring.

Just for Fun

- Put some old pennies that have lost their shine on a plate. Sprinkle a little salt on each penny and then add a few drops of vinegar. Presto! You have pennies that shine like new.

In this chapter, you have investigated a number of chemical reactions. In the next two chapters, you will explore two general types of chemical reactions. These reactions are basically the same for many substances. For example, in Chapter 5 you will investigate the reaction between vinegar and ammonia, which is similar to the reaction between hydrochloric acid and lye (sodium hydroxide). Both are acid-base reactions.

The reaction between iron and oxygen to form rust, which you will use in Chapter 6, is similar to the reaction between hydrogen and oxygen to form water. The rates of these two reactions are very different. Hydrogen *burns* in oxygen, while iron reacts very slowly with oxygen. Nevertheless, both involve the combination of a substance with oxygen—a process called oxidation.

5

Acid + Base: A Colorful Chemical Reaction

In the last chapter, you examined some chemical reactions—reactions in which new substances are formed. One very common type of chemical reaction is that between an acid and a base. The word acid comes from the Latin *acidus*, which means sharp or sour. Historically, substances that tasted sour came to be known as acids. Gradually, acids were identified as substances that: (1) taste sour; (2) dissolve in water to form solutions that conduct electricity; (3) contain hydrogen that is released when the acid is added to certain metals, such as zinc; (4) turn blue litmus red; and (5) *neutralize* bases. Neutralize means to change to a substance that is neither acid nor base.

Testing the Definition of Acids

Many acids are poisonous so you should not taste them. But you know from experience that lemon juice and vinegar taste sour. Therefore, from the definition of an acid, you might expect that these substances are acids. If they are, they should conduct electricity. Experiments, like the ones you can find in another book in this series called *Science Projects About Electricity and Magnets,* show that sulfuric acid conducts electricity very well, whereas water is a poor conductor. Vinegar, like lemon juice, is a fair, but not good conductor. For this and for other reasons, sulfuric acid is called a *strong acid,* while vinegar and lemon juice are called *weak acids.*

These and other acids react with zinc to form a gas. If the gas is used to blow bubbles in a soap solution, the bubbles will ascend into the air like a hot air balloon. This happens because the gas produced is hydrogen, which is less dense than air. If a burning match is brought close to one of the gas-filled bubbles, the bubble will burn!

Bases: The Counterpart of Acids

You will have a chance to explore the other properties that characterize acids in this chapter. But before you do, you need to consider bases, the second type of substances mentioned in the title of this chapter. Another name for bases is *alkalies.* This word comes from the medieval Latin word *alcali,* which means ashes. As you might guess, ashes have the properties that have come to characterize alkaline substances or bases. In general, bases are substances that have a bitter taste and feel slippery, like soap. [It may not surprise you to learn that early American settlers made soap by boiling animal fat with the lye obtained from leaching (washing) wood ashes.] Bases also are conductors of electricity, turn red litmus blue, and neutralize acids. **Many bases are poisonous so you should not taste them.**

In the next few investigations you will have a chance to explore the properties of acids and bases. You will learn how acids and bases can be identified in colorful ways and how they can neutralize one another.

5.1 Identifying Acids and Bases with Litmus*

As you read above, acids turn blue litmus red and bases turn red litmus blue. Your school's science supplies probably include some litmus paper strips. Litmus paper is an acid-base *indicator* because it can be used to tell which substances are acids and which are bases. Ask your science teacher if you may have a few pieces of litmus paper of each color. You will not need many because, as you will see, there are other indicators that can be substituted for litmus. If your school does not have litmus paper, you can buy some at a hobby store or at one of the scientific supply houses listed in the appendix. If you are unable to obtain litmus paper, you can go on to the next investigation where you will make your own indicator.

Pour a few milliliters of vinegar into a small jar or a test tube. If you use a jar, dip a piece of blue litmus paper into the vinegar. If you use a test tube, use an eyedropper or a glass stirring rod to remove a drop of vinegar from the tube. Add the drop to a piece of blue litmus paper.

Things you'll need:

- red and blue strips of litmus paper
- vinegar
- small jars, such as baby food or jelly jars or test tubes
- eyedropper or glass stirring rod
- clear household ammonia
- lemon juice
- apple juice
- grapefruit juice
- cleanser powder (in water)
- water
- rubbing alcohol
- salt solution
- sugar solution
- aspirin (in water)
- wood ashes (in water)
- baking soda (in water)
- baking powder (in water)
- limewater (calcium oxide)
- citric acid or Kool-Aid crystals (in water)
- washing soda (in water)

Does the litmus turn red? What happens if you repeat the experiment with red litmus paper?

You could leach wood ashes to obtain a base, but it is much easier to use a clear solution of household ammonia, which is also a well known base. Pour a few milliliters of the ammonia solution into a small jar or a test tube. Test as before, first with red and then with blue litmus paper. Which litmus paper changes color?

Now use your litmus paper to test the other materials listed under "Things you'll need." (Save these materials. You will use them again in later investigations.) Where necessary, add water to make a solution that can be tested. Which of these substances are acids? Which are bases? Which have no effect on either red or blue litmus paper? These substances are said to be neutral.

During project 4.6, you were asked to save the white solid (magnesium hydroxide) that you collected. Place the solid in a small jar or test tube and add a few milliliters of water. Is the magnesium hydroxide very soluble in water?

Test the mixture of magnesium hydroxide and water with litmus paper. Is it acidic, basic, or neutral? Save this mixture for testing with other indicators.

5.2 Other Acid-Base Indicators*

If you have ever added lemon to tea and seen the change in color, you know that tea is an acid-base indicator. There are many natural acid-base indicators. In this investigation you will explore four of them.

Cabbage juice

A natural and very effective acid-base indicator is the juice in red cabbage. You can extract this juice quite easily. Remove a few leaves from a red cabbage. Break the leaves into small pieces and place them in a non–aluminum pot together with some water. Put a cover on the pot and **ask an adult to help you heat the pot until the water is boiling.** Reduce the heat, but continue boiling for about half an hour. Then turn off the heat and let the water cool to room temperature. Remove the cabbage leaves with forceps. Pour the cabbage juice solution into a container and cover it. The purple cabbage juice extract should be stored in a refrigerator. You will be using it here and in other experiments.

Things you'll need:

• red cabbage
• non-aluminum cooking pot and cover
• water
• forceps
• eyedropper
• small jars, such as baby food or jelly jars or test tubes
• white vinegar
• clear household ammonia
• lemon juice
• apple juice
• grapefruit juice
• rubbing alcohol
• cleanser powder (in water)
• salt solution
• sugar solution
• aspirin (in water)
• wood ashes (in water)
• baking soda (in water)
• baking powder (in water)
• lime (calcium oxide) (in water)
• citric acid or Kool-Aid crystals (in water)
• washing soda (in water)

(list continued on next page)

Add a few drops of the cabbage extract to several milliliters of white vinegar in a small glass jar or test tube. What is the color of the cabbage juice indicator in an acid?

Now add a few drops of the cabbage juice to a few milliliters of ammonia. What is the color of the cabbage juice indicator in a base?

Add a few drops of the indicator to some tap water. What is the color of the indicator in a neutral solution?

Things you'll need: (con't)
- magnesium hydroxide (from investigation 4.6 and 5.1)
- unsweetened grape juice
- laxative pills that contain phenolphthalein
- heavy cup
- spoon
- 1-quart cooking pot

From the tests you did using litmus paper in project 5.1, predict the color of drops of your cabbage juice indicator in lemon juice, apple juice, grapefruit juice, alcohol, cleanser powder (in water), salt and sugar solutions, crushed aspirin dissolved in water, wood ashes mixed with water, solutions of baking soda and baking powder, limewater (calcium oxide), citric acid or Kool-Aid crystals dissolved in water, magnesium hydroxide, and washing soda crystals (in water). If you did not do project 5.1, determine whether each of these substances is an acid, a base, or neutral.

Unsweetened Grape Juice

Unsweetened red grape juice is another substance that can be used as an acid-base indicator. It too should be stored in a refrigerator. You will be using it again in other experiments. Add a few drops of unsweetened grape juice to several milliliters of white vinegar in a small glass jar or test tube. What is the color of grape juice indicator in an acid?

Now add a few drops of grape juice to a few milliliters of ammonia. What is the color of grape juice indicator in a base?

Add a few drops of grape juice to some tap water. What is the color of grape juice indicator in a neutral solution? Why is cabbage juice a better indicator than grape juice?

From the tests you did using litmus paper or using cabbage juice, predict the color of drops of grape juice in lemon juice and all the other substances you tested before.

Turmeric

A third natural indicator can be found in turmeric, a common spice. To prepare an extract of turmeric, stir about 1/4 teaspoonful of turmeric into 50 mL (0.25 cup) of rubbing alcohol. Save this extract for use in this and in other experiments.

Add a few drops of turmeric extract to several milliliters of white vinegar in a small glass jar or test tube. What is the color of the turmeric indicator in an acid?

Now add several drops of turmeric to a few milliliters of ammonia. What is the color of this indicator in a base?

Add a few drops of the indicator to some tap water. What is the color of turmeric indicator in a neutral solution? Why is cabbage juice a better indicator than turmeric?

Again, based on your findings with other indicators, predict the color of turmeric indicator when added to the various substances you have tested before.

Phenolphthalein

Examine the list of ingredients on laxative pills. Some of them contain phenolphthalein, which can be used as an indicator. To prepare an extract of phenolphthalein, place a laxative pill in a heavy cup. Crush the laxative pill with the back of a spoon. Then add about 50 mL (1.7 oz) of rubbing alcohol to the powder. Stir the mixture thoroughly to dissolve as much phenolphthalein as possible. Pour the liquid into a small jar or beaker leaving any undissolved solid in the cup. **Be sure**

to rinse the cup and spoon thoroughly when you are through. Rubbing alcohol is poisonous.

Add a few drops of phenolphthalein extract to several milliliters of ammonia in a small glass jar or test tube. What is the color of the indicator in a base?

Now add several drops of the indicator to a few milliliters of vinegar. What is the color of phenolphthalein in an acid?

Next, add the indicator to some tap water. What is the color of phenolphthalein in a neutral solution? How is phenolphthalein similar to turmeric as an indicator? How is it different?

Again, based on your findings with other indicators, predict the color of phenolphthalein extract when added to the various substances you have tested before.

5.3 Indicator Papers and Sticks*

You can prepare indicator papers, similar to litmus paper, or indicator sticks using some of the indicator solutions you prepared before. Cut rectangular strips from the coffee filters or from filter paper. Dip the strips into solutions of your turmeric extract, grape juice, or cabbage juice and place them on paper towels to dry. You can also dip the ends of cotton swabs into the solutions. Then place the swab sticks on top of small tin cans so that the cotton swabs extend into the air where they can dry.

Things you'll need:
- cabbage juice (from project 5.2)
- unsweetened grape juice (from project 5.2)
- turmeric extract (from project 5.2)
- coffee filters or filter paper
- cotton swabs
- various acids, bases, and neutral substances (from projects 5.1 and 5.2)

If you prefer, you can divide your indicator solutions in half. Add a few drops of vinegar to one set to color the cabbage juice and grape juices red (the turmeric will remain yellow). To the second set, add a few drops of ammonia to turn the cabbage and grape juices green and the turmeric red. Now you can have two sets of paper strips for each indicator. You can use them just as you used red and blue litmus paper.

If you use what you have discovered to complete the table on the next page, you will find it helpful. Keep it in your notebook for ready reference. **Do not write in this book.**

Test your various indicators in the same substances you used in experiments 5.1 and 5.2. If you could use only one indicator, which one would you choose? Why?

Exploring on Your Own

- Read the label on a bottle of vitamin C tablets. Then crush one of the tablets into a powder and add some water. Divide the solution into four parts. Predict the color of litmus paper, drops of cabbage juice, drops of grape juice, and drops of turmeric extract when added to a solution of vitamin C.

Indicator	In acid	In base	In neutral
Red Litmus	Remains red	Turns blue	Remains red
Blue Litmus	Turns red	Remains blue	Remains blue
Red cabbage juice			
Green cabbage juice			
Red grape juice			
Green grape juice			
Yellow turmeric			
Red turmeric			

Just for Fun

- Tell your friends that you can change red grape juice to mint juice and back to grape juice. But before you do, dilute 20 mL (0.7 of unsweetened grape juice with 180 mL (6 oz) of water to reduce the intensity of the color. Pour the diluted juice into a glass. In a second glass, place a few drops of ammonia solution. When you pour the grape juice into the glass, it will turn green because ammonia is a base. In a third glass, place enough vinegar ahead of time to change the color back to red. (You will need to practice to get the right amounts of ammonia and vinegar.) When you pour the green "mint" into the third glass it turns back to grape juice.

5.4 Neutralization*

You remember that one characteristic of an acid was its ability to neutralize a base. Similarly, one characteristic of a base is its ability to neutralize an acid. To see what this means, you will have to add an acid to a base or a base to an acid.

Pour about 10 mL (0.3 oz) of vinegar into a small jar or beaker. Add a few drops of cabbage juice. Stir the mixture to obtain a uniform color. Then use an eyedropper to add ammonia drop by drop to the vinegar. Notice what happens to the color of the solution in the region where the ammonia lands. Stir the liquid as you add the drops until you see a distinct color change. What has happened?

Things you'll need:

- white vinegar
- small jars such as baby food or jelly jars or beakers
- cabbage juice indicator
- plastic spoon or glass stirring rod
- eyedropper
- household ammonia
- baking soda

Now go the other way. Rinse your eyedropper and use it to add drops of vinegar to the solution. Do this slowly. Notice the effect of one drop on the color of the solution. Can you see an intermediate color (purple) just before the solution changes from acid to base or base to acid? Remember, cabbage juice is purple in a neutral substance. If you can see the indicator turn purple, you are witnessing the exact point at which neutralization occurs.

What happens to the color of the neutral solution if you add a drop or two of vinegar? What happens if you add a drop or two of ammonia?

You have seen that just a drop or two of an acid or a base can make a neutral solution acidic or basic. But suppose you have something that reacts with the acid. What will happen then? To find out, add some water to a teaspoonful of baking soda in a small jar or beaker. Add a few drops of the indicator to the baking soda. Now slowly add vinegar to the solution. Once you reach the neutralization point, is the color change from neutral to acidic sudden or gradual?

Exploring on Your Own

- Cut 3 flat slices from an apple. Place them on a paper towel. Spread some citric acid or Kool-Aid crystals on one piece. Crush a vitamin C tablet (ascorbic acid) and spread it on the second piece. Leave the third piece exposed to the air as a control. Watch these pieces over a 24 hour period. What effect do these acids have on the browning process that occurs when apples are cut and exposed to the oxygen in air? See if you can predict what effect lemon juice would have on the browning reaction. Do you see why apples in a fruit salad that contains grapefruit, oranges, or other citrus fruits do not turn brown?

Strong and Weak Acids and Bases

At the beginning of this chapter, you read that sulfuric acid is a stronger acid than vinegar. This was revealed by the fact that sulfuric acid was a better conductor of electricity than vinegar. The degree of acidity of a substance can be determined by its pH, which measures the amount of hydrogen ion provided by the acid to conduct electricity. The pH of a substance can be measured with pH paper. This is a kind of "litmus paper" paper. However, pH paper has been soaked in a number of different acid-base indicators. Litmus paper changes from one color to another at the neutralization point—a pH of 7. But these other indicators change color at different degrees of acidity. Neutral substances have a pH of 7. Substances with a pH less than 7 are acidic. A solution with a pH of 1 is very acidic; one with a pH of 5 is mildly acidic. Substances with a pH greater than 7 are basic. A solution with a pH of 14 is very basic; one with a pH of 9 is mildly basic.

During project 5.5, you will have a chance to test the pH of a number of substances.

5.5 pH, the Degree of Acidity*

As you know the pH scale measures the degree of acidity. You can measure the pH of various substances using pH paper. Ask your science teacher if you may borrow some pH paper and the color scale that goes with it. If your school does not have pH paper, you may be able to buy some at a hobby shop, a pool supply company (pH paper can be used to measure the acidity of swimming pool water), or a science supply company.

Use the pH paper to test the acidity of the substances listed under materials needed **except for the**

Things you'll need:

- pH paper and color scale
- vinegar
- small jars or beakers
- water
- ammonia
- cleanser powder (in water)
- baking soda (in water)
- lemon juice
- grape juice
- washing soda (in water)
- hydrochloric acid solution
- sodium hydroxide solution

hydrochloric acid and the sodium hydroxide. Were you surprised to find that the pH of water was probably not 7? Most water, including rain water, is slightly acidic.

What happens to the pH of vinegar if you dilute it by adding 10 mL (0.3 oz) of vinegar to 90 mL (3 oz) of water? What happens to the pH of the vinegar if you continue diluting it 1/10 with water? What happens to the pH of ammonia if you dilute it in the same way with water?

Ask your science teacher to help you test dilute (1.0 Molar) hydrochloric acid and dilute (1.0 Molar) sodium hydroxide with pH paper. **Be sure you do this only in the presence of your science teacher.** What is the pH of these solutions?

Exploring on Your Own

- Use pH paper to measure the acidity of rain water. Does the pH of the rain water in a long-lasting storm change with time? Is the pH of the rain water related to the size of the drops? Collect some snow and let it melt. What is the pH of snow? In a long-lasting snow storm, does the pH of the snow change with time?

- Make two miniature "lakes" by pouring water into two wide soup bowls. What is the pH of the water in the two bowls? Pour some fine sand into one bowl; add an equal amount of limestone (calcium carbonate) to the other. What is the pH in each bowl after these solids have been added? Add ten drops of vinegar to each lake. What is the pH in each lake after the vinegar has been added? Continue adding vinegar and measuring the pH. What do you find to be different about these two lakes? Based on your investigation, would a lake with a sandy bottom or one with a limestone bottom be most affected by acid rain?

- Design an experiment to test the effect of pH on the germination of radish and bean seeds. Bear in mind that seeds will germinate on damp paper towels. Vinegar can be used to make tap water more acidic. Lime can be used to make tap water more alkaline.

In this chapter you have investigated a reaction that is basically the same for all acids and bases. In the next chapter, you will examine another kind of general reaction that is similar for the many different substances that react with oxygen.

6

Oxidation: Reactions with Oxygen

In Chapter 2, you learned that oxygen makes up 21 percent of the atmosphere. It is also the most abundant element in the earth's crust (46 percent). Water, which covers two-thirds of the earth, is 89 percent oxygen by weight. Sand (silicon dioxide) is 53 percent oxygen. Unlike nitrogen, which is relatively unreactive, oxygen is very reactive. It is found combined with a great many other elements to form compounds such as iron oxide, aluminum oxide, calcium oxide, calcium carbonate, and so on. It is the rapid combination of oxygen with such things as wood, oil, and coal that is responsible for the heat and light (flames) you see when these substances burn.

The combination of oxygen with other substances is called oxidation. In Chapter 4, you found that the iron acetate you obtained by placing steel wool in vinegar reacted with ammonia to form a green slime—ferrous hydroxide. Remember how the green slime turned yellowish and then brown as it sat on the filter paper? The green hydroxide was reacting with the oxygen in the air to form another brownish hydroxide of iron—ferric hydroxide. What you saw was one example of an oxidation reaction.

Sometimes an oxidation reaction is rapid, as it is when substances burn; sometimes it is slow, as it is when iron and other metals rust. Experiment 6.1 will give you a chance to see how the rate of rusting is affected by various chemicals you have used before.

6.1 Comparing Rusting Rates*

You know that iron will rust. This happens when oxygen in the air slowly combines with iron to form a compound called iron oxide (rust). The rate at which iron rusts often depends on the acidity of the environment around the iron. To see

Things you'll need:

- steel wool (no soap)
- vinegar
- ammonia
- paper towel

how several different chemicals may affect the rate of rusting, cut a steel wool pad (one without soap) into four equal parts. Soak one piece in water, another in ammonia, and a third in vinegar. Leave the fourth piece dry as a control. After the steel wool samples have soaked for several minutes, remove them and place them on labeled paper towels. **Then wash your hands thoroughly.**

Leave the samples for about 24 hours. Check them periodically to see what happens. You may find rust stains on the paper towel, as well as on the steel wool. Which piece begins to rust first? Which one or ones seem not to rust at all? Does acidity have any effect on the rusting rate of iron?

Burning: Rapid Oxidation

Rusting is an example of slow oxidation. In the next few investigations, you will be using burning candles, which is an example of fast oxidation. **Because you will be using matches and flames in these investigations, be sure you work only under the supervision of an adult. If you have long hair, tie it back** so there is no danger that it will catch on fire.

6.2 Burning Birthday Candles*

Stand several birthday candles in a row on small tin can lids or pennies as shown in Figure 6-1. You can support them with melted wax from a candle or with small lumps of clay. Check the jars to be sure that they fit over the candles. If the smallest jar is so short that the candle flame will touch it, you may have to cut the candle. **Under adult supervision use a match to light the candles.**

Things you'll need:
- birthday candles
- matches
- melted wax or clay
- small tin can lids or pennies
- an assortment of jars or beakers of different sizes
- cobalt chloride paper (blue)
- limewater

Once the candles are burning, cover each, in turn, with a different size jar or beaker. Use a clock or a watch with a second hand to measure the time that each candle burns before going out. How do the times compare? Is the time that the candle burns related to the size of the jar? How can you explain this relationship?

When a candle burns, there is good evidence for a chemical reaction. After all, the candle burns away and there is a flame. But what are the products—the new substances that form? You may have noticed some droplets of liquid on the inside surface of the jars or beakers you placed over the burning candles. Those droplets are water.

Check to see if your school science supplies include *blue* cobalt chloride paper. Your science teacher may let you have some. Then you will be able to test the droplets yourself. If the cobalt chloride paper has turned pink, **ask your teacher to help you change the paper strips back to blue by heating them.** Then simply touch a blue paper strip to the droplets. You will see that the paper turns pink. Now touch another paper to a droplet of water. What happens to the color of the cobalt chloride paper? Is water produced when a candle burns?

To see if there is a gaseous product, burn a candle again. But this time place a flask or a bottle with a narrow neck over the candle. After the candle goes out, pour about 20 mL (0.7 oz) of limewater (see project 4.5) into the bottle or flask and swirl it around. Pour an identical amount of limewater into a bottle or flask that has only air in it. This bottle serves as a control in your experiment. Did either bottle contain carbon dioxide? Is carbon dioxide produced when a candle burns?

Exploring on Your Own

- Is the time that a candle burns in a container proportional to the volume of the air in the container? That is, if you double the volume of the container, will the candle burn twice as long? If you triple the

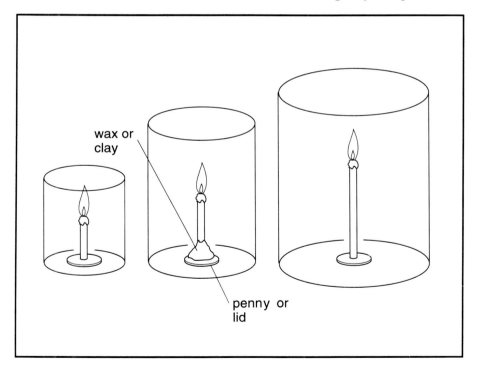

Figure 6-1) How is the time that a candle will burn related to the size of the container in which it is burning?

volume, will it burn three times as long? Design an experiment to find out. **Then carry out your experiment under adult supervision.**

An Hypothesis

Perhaps the reason that a candle burns longer in a larger jar is that the larger jar contains more oxygen. After the oxygen is used up, the candle goes out. Since a bigger jar holds more air, it also holds more oxygen.

Jan van Helmont (1577–1644) performed an experiment in the seventeenth century that shows that not all the oxygen is used up when a candle burns. He placed a burning candle and a mouse in a large jar. He then sealed the jar and waited. The candle soon burned out, but the mouse continued sniffing about for quite some time before van Helmont opened the jar. If the candle had used up *all* the oxygen, the mouse could not have survived in the jar. Animals cannot live without oxygen!

Van Helmont's experiment reveals that there must be oxygen in the jars when the candles go out. But if there is oxygen in the jars why do the candles go out?

You can use the reaction between iron (steel wool) and oxygen to see how much oxygen there is in air. Then perhaps you will be able to do another experiment to see how much oxygen is left after a candle burns.

6.3 What Fraction of Air is Oxygen?*

Soak a pad of steel wool (one without soap) in a jar or beaker of vinegar for a few minutes. While the steel wool is soaking, fill a large pan or shallow container to a depth of about 2 cm (1 in) with water. To make the water more visible, you might like to add a few drops of food coloring.

Pull a few strands of steel wool from the pad that has soaked in vinegar. Roll them into a small, loosely packed ball. Make three such balls of steel wool. These balls should be slightly wider than the diameter of the narrow jars (olive jars are good) or test tubes you plan to use. Put a steel wool ball into each of three tall narrow jars or

Things you'll need:

- steel wool (without soap)
- jar or beaker
- large pan or other shallow container
- water
- food coloring (optional)
- vinegar
- small jar such as baby food jar or beaker
- four tall narrow jars, such as olive jars or large test tubes
- pencil
- small sheet of paper
- marking pen or rubber band
- ruler

large test tubes. Use a pencil to push one ball all the way to the bottom of the jar or tube. Push a second ball about three-fourths of the way to the bottom of another tube or jar, and push a third ball about half–way down a third tube. Wad a small piece of paper into a ball and push it to the bottom of the fourth jar or tube.

Turn these tubes upside down and place them side by side in the pan of water you prepared earlier. See Figure 6-2. If need be, devise some means of fastening the tubes so they will not tip over. Leave the inverted tubes for a period of 24 hours. After that, mark the water level in each tube with a marking pen or a rubber band. Leave them for several more hours to see if the water level rises any higher. Once the water level has stopped rising, look closely at the steel wool in the

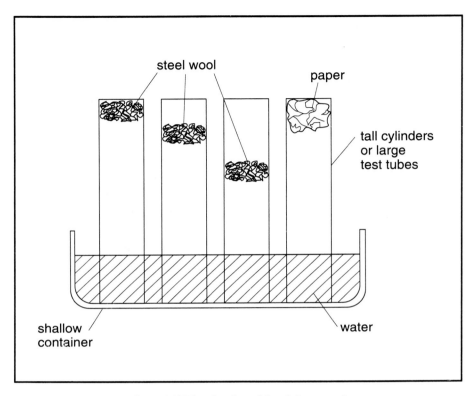

Figure 6-2)What fraction of the air is oxygen?

tubes. How has it changed? Then compare the water levels in the tubes. In which tube has the water risen little, if at all? Why did the water not rise in this tube?

Compare the water levels in the other three tubes. Are they about the same? Does the position of the steel wool seem to have any effect?

Use the ruler to measure the height of the water in each of the three tubes that contained steel wool. In each case, what is the ratio of the height of the water level to the total height of the tube? What fraction of the air is oxygen according to your measurements with each tube? How do these values compare with the percentage of oxygen in air given at the beginning of this chapter?

A Time for Reflection and Comparison

If you did project 6.3 with care, you probably found that your results in the three tubes were quite consistent. That is, the water level rose by about the same fraction of the total height in each tube. If possible, you might compare your results with others who did the same experiment. Did they get similar results? Were their results consistent?

The fraction of the air that is oxygen, which was given as 21 percent at the beginning of this chapter, was obtained from a variety of experiments. It is probably quite close to the fraction you obtained in project 6.3. In your experiment, the air in the jar was sealed off from the rest of the air by the water at the bottom of the tube. Consequently, your results indicate that when steel wool rusts in a closed container, it combines with nearly *all* the oxygen in the air, given enough time.

In the next investigation you will replace the slowly rusting steel wool with the burning candle. Will you again obtain similar results?

6.4 The Reaction of a Burning Candle and Air*

Fill a large pan or shallow container to a depth of about 2 cm (1 in) with water. To make the water more visible, you might like to add a few drops of food coloring. Make four small clay holders for birthday candles. Place them on the bottom of the pan or shallow container. Place a birthday candle in each one. **With an adult to help you, light each candle.** Now place the four tubes you used before over the candles. Vary the time it takes you to bring the open end of the tube down over the candle.

Things you'll need:

- large pan or other shallow container
- water
- food coloring (optional
- clay
- birthday candles
- matches
- four tall narrow jars, such as olive jars or large test tubes
- ruler

How long does it take for the water levels to reach their maximum heights in this experiment? Measure the height of the water in each of the four tubes. In each case, how does it compare with the total height of the tube? Is it the same in each case? Does the amount of water that enters the tube seem to be related to the time it took you to lower the tube down over the candle?

Assuming the candle uses all the oxygen in the sealed off air when it burns, what fraction of the air is oxygen according to your results from each tube? Are your results consistent?

Another Look at Consistency

You probably found that your results in project 6.4 were not very consistent. You may even have obtained data suggesting that oxygen makes up more than 25 percent of the air. How can your results in project 6.4 be reconciled with those in project 6.3 and with Jan van Helmont's experiment?

When you bring a closed tube down over a burning candle, it seems likely that the air in the tube might expand. If the air expands, where will it go? It might bubble out the bottom of the tube. Then, after the candle goes out, the air in the tube will cool and contract. As it does, air pressure would push water in the shallow container up into the tube. The time it takes you to bring the tube down over the candle might affect the amount of the air that is left to expand when the tube reaches the water. This, in turn, would affect the amount of air that reenters the tube when it cools. Consequently, the results might vary quite a bit.

In project 6.5, you can test this hypothesis that tries to explain the inconsistencies you found in the last experiment. First, you will add a little soap to the water to see if you can detect bubbles coming from under the tube. Then you will cover the burning candle with a tube that has a flexible membrane to see if you can detect the expansion and contraction of the air due to heating and cooling.

6.5 Checking the Inconsistency Hypothesis*

Fill a large pan or shallow container to a depth of about 2 cm (1 in) with water. Add a little soap to the water and stir to mix it thoroughly. The soap will cause bubbles to form if air is pushed out the tube. To make the water more visible, you might like to add a few drops of food coloring.

Make a small clay holder for the birthday candle and place it on the bottom of the pan or shallow container. **With an adult to help you, light the candle.** Quickly place the tube over the candle. Can you see any bubbles due to air expanding out the bottom of the tube?

If you do not see any bubbles, it may be that the hypothesis is wrong, or it may be that the air expanded out the tube before it reached the water. If you use a larger tube, it is less likely that the gas would all expand before the tube reaches the water. So if you did not see bubbles, try using one of the large jars or beakers you used in project 6.2. **Ask an adult to help you light the candle and supervise the rest of this experiment.** Then bring the large jar or beaker down quickly over the burning candle. Do you see bubbles coming out from under the opening in the jar?

To see if the air contracts after it expands, you will need a glass or plastic tube open at both ends, or a small frozen juice can from which both top and bottom have been removed. The tube should be wide

Things you'll need:

- large pan or other shallow container
- water
- soap
- food coloring (optional)
- clay
- birthday candle
- matches
- tall narrow jar, such as olive jar or large test tube
- food coloring (optional)
- large jar or beaker
- wide glass or plastic tube *open* at *both ends* or a small frozen juice can open at both ends
- rubber balloon
- shears
- rubber band

enough to fit easily over the burning candle without touching the flame. A diameter of 3 cm (1.25 in) is good, but you may have to use something a little larger or smaller. It should be tall enough so that the candle's flame does not touch the rubber membrane that you are going to stretch across the top of the tube. If the tube is too short, you can use a shorter candle—one that has been used or one that has been cut off.

Make a disk from clay or plasticine. The diameter of the disk should be larger than the diameter of the open tube you are going to place over the candle. Then cut off the bottom half of a rubber balloon and stretch it across the top of the tube. Use a rubber band to keep it stretched and in place as shown in Figure 6-3.

With an adult to help you, put a candle in the center of the disk and light it. Once the candle is burning well, bring the tube down quickly over the burning candle and press it into the clay so that no air can escape out the bottom of the tube. What happens to the rubber membrane? Does it stretch outward at first? Does it then move into the tube as the air cools and contracts?

Repeat this experiment several times. Each time, vary the speed at which you bring the tube down over the candle. Does the rate at which you lower the tube affect the amount that the membrane moves outward and inward?

Do the results of this experiment seem to confirm your hypothesis about the inconsistency of the results in project 6.4?

A Prediction

The results of project 6.5 probably showed you why the results were so different when you placed a closed tube over a burning candle in water. The time it takes to lower the tube over the candle determines how much the air will expand after it is closed off. If the air is hot when it is sealed off, it will not expand much more. If it is still cool when it is sealed off, it will expand a lot. This, in turn, determines how much

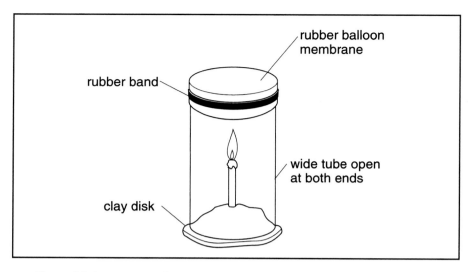

Figure 6-3 Apparatus used to see if the air around a burning candle expands and contracts.

the air will contract when it cools. If it has expanded a lot, it will contract a lot and vice versa. When the tube is lowered rapidly, the air is heated and expands *after* it reaches the water. Therefore, there are plenty of bubbles because most of the expansion occurs after the mouth of the tube is under water. A slowly lowered tube, on the other hand, will produce few, if any, bubbles because the air has already expanded by the time the tube reaches the water.

But what about van Helmont's experiment with the mouse? Does a burning candle use up all the oxygen in the tube? Assume for the moment that the candle does not use up all the oxygen. If that is true, then you would predict that there is still oxygen in the tube after the candle has gone out. To check your prediction, you can place some steel wool in a tube and lower it over a burning candle in water. **Ask an adult to help.** After the candle goes out, the steel wool should continue to react with the oxygen and the water level should rise over a 24 hour period. In fact, by measuring how much the water level rises, you can find out how much oxygen was left in the tube after the candle burned. You will test your prediction in project 6.6.

6.6 Testing a Prediction*

To test your hypothesis, repeat the experiment you did in project 6.4 once more **with adult help**. But this time, push a small ball of steel wool that has been rinsed with vinegar to the bottom of each of the four tall, narrow jars or test tubes before inverting each one over a burning candle. When the candle goes out and water stops rising in the tube, mark the water level on the tube with a marking pen or a rubber band (Figure 6-4).

Watch the water levels in the tubes over the next 24 hours. Look closely at the steel wool. Is there evidence that it has reacted? Does

Things you'll need:

- steel wool
- four tall narrow jars, such as olive jars or large test tubes
- vinegar
- jar or beaker
- birthday candles
- clay
- matches
- marking pen or rubber bands
- ruler

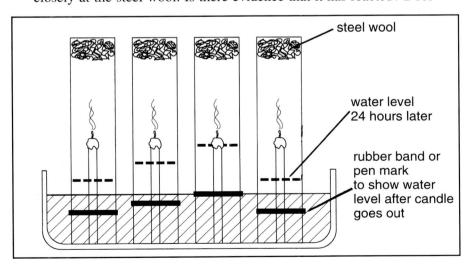

Figure 6-4) An experiment to find out how much of the oxygen in air is consumed by a candle before it goes out.

the water level rise in each tube? Does it *rise* by the same amount in each tube? Use your ruler to measure the *change* in the water level. How does the change in the water level here compare with the rise in water level that you found when only steel wool (no candle) was used in project 6.3?

Do the results of this experiment confirm your prediction? Did the candle use up *all* of the oxygen in the jar when it burned? Based on your results, what fraction of the oxygen in the jar was used by the candle before it went out?

Another Look at a Burning Candle

Your results in investigation 6.6 indicate that a candle goes out well before it has used up all the available oxygen. While an animal, such as van Helmont's mouse, can continue to breathe in air that has less than 21 percent oxygen, a candle cannot burn. When the percentage of oxygen in the air becomes less than about 16 percent, it is not concentrated enough to sustain the rapid oxidation of a burning candle. But suppose the concentration of oxygen were greater than 21 percent. Would burning be more rapid than usual? You can find out by doing experiment 6.7.

6.7 Making and Testing Oxygen*

To make oxygen gas, you can break up hydrogen peroxide, a compound of hydrogen and oxygen. To do this, put about 1/8 teaspoonful of potassium iodide in a flask or a soda bottle. Your science teacher may be able to provide the potassium iodide. Add about 75 mL (3 oz) of 3 percent hydrogen peroxide.

You will use a balloon to collect the gas produced just as you did in project 4.5 when you made carbon dioxide. You may remember that this can be done by placing a balloon over a one-hole rubber stopper attached to one end of the glass or plastic tube as shown in Figure 4-4a. The one-hole rubber stopper at the other end of the tube should fit the neck of a small soda bottle or flask where the gas will be produced. Insert the stopper into the neck of the flask or bottle (Figure 6-5) and swirl the flask or bottle to mix the solid and liquid. What evidence do you have that a chemical reaction is taking place? What happens to the rate at which oxygen is produced as the reaction proceeds?

Things you'll need:

- potassium iodide
- small flask or soda bottle
- 3% hydrogen peroxide solution
- balloons (see project 4.5)
- two one-hole rubber stoppers, one should fit the mouth of the flask or bottle and short length of glass or plastic tubing (see project 4.5)
- small wide-mouth bottle or jar
- pan
- water
- matches
- wood splint or wooden coffee stirrer
- tie band (twist tie)
- limewater
- small jar or test tube
- acid-base indicator
- balance (see project 1.3)

When the reaction is over and the balloon stops expanding, seal the neck of the balloon with your thumb and finger. Remove the glass or plastic tube from the lower stopper and place the end of it under a

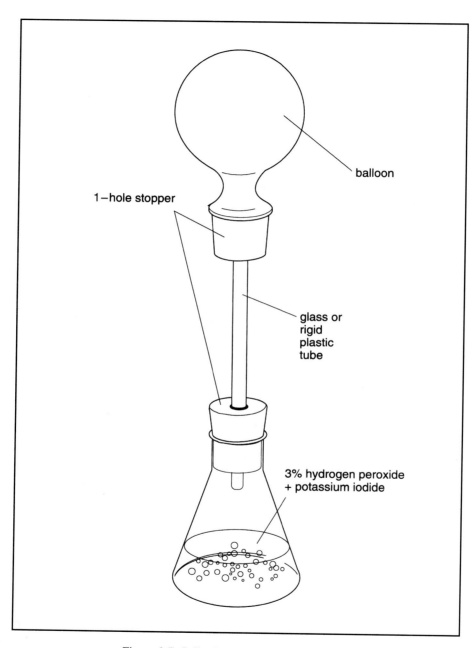

balloon

1-hole stopper

glass or
rigid
plastic
tube

3% hydrogen peroxide
+ potassium iodide

Figure 6-5) Collecting oxygen gas in a balloon.

small water-filled bottle or jar that is upside down in a pan of water as shown in Figure 6-6a. Let the gas bubble up into the jar displacing the water. (If you have any gas left after the bottle is full, tie off the neck of the balloon with a tie band so you can save it for some other tests.) **Ask an adult to help you light the wood splint and test the gas.** When the splint is burning well, blow it out. The end of the splint should be glowing, but not in flames. Remove the bottle of gas from the water, turn it right side up and lower the glowing splint into the upper end of the bottle as shown in Figure 6-6b. What happens? Does oxygen make the wood burn faster? Remove the wood splint and extinguish it in the pan of water.

If you have some oxygen left in the balloon, release a few bubbles into about 10 mL (0.3 oz) of limewater in a small jar or test tube. Does the limewater turn milky? If you bubble oxygen into water, does the water become acidic, basic, or remain neutral? How can you find out?

If you collect one or more balloonfuls of oxygen, you can use the balance you built in investigation 1.3 to compare the density of oxygen with the densities of other gases. Which is denser, oxygen or carbon dioxide? Oxygen or air? Oxygen or "lung air"?

Exploring on Your Own

- With a setup like the one you used in project 6.7, measure the volume of gas released when 1/8 teaspoonful of potassium iodide reacts with 75 mL (3 oz) of 3 percent hydrogen peroxide. Then repeat the experiment using twice as much potassium iodide. Is the reaction faster? Does the volume of the oxygen produced double? If you use 150 mL (5 oz) of 3 percent hydrogen peroxide, is the reaction faster? Does the volume of oxygen produced double?

- Will there be a reaction if you do not add potassium iodide to the hydrogen peroxide?

- Pour a few milliliters of 3 percent hydrogen peroxide into a small jar, bottle, flask, or a test tube. Do you see any evidence of a chemical reaction? Now add a slice of raw potato to the liquid. Is there evidence of a chemical reaction now? From project 6.7, you might think that the gas being released here is oxygen. Figure out a way to collect some of the gas in a bottle or jar. Once you have collected the gas, **ask an adult to help you test the gas with a glowing wood splint**. Is the gas oxygen?

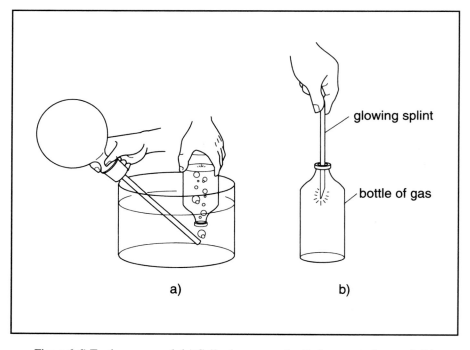

Figure 6-6) Testing oxygen. 6-6a) Collecting oxygen by displacement of water. 6-6b) Testing the gas with a glowing wood splint.

APPENDIX
Suppliers of Materials

Carolina Biological Supply Co.
2700 York Road
Burlington, NC 27215
(800) 334-5551;
http://www.carolina.com

Central Scientific Co. (CENCO)
3300 Cenco Parkway
Franklin Park, IL 60131
(800) 262-3626;
http://www.cenconet.com

Connecticut Valley Biological
Supply Co., Inc.
82 Valley Road, Box 326
Southampton, MA 01073
(800) 628-7748

Delta Education
P.O. Box 915
Hudson, NH 03051-0915
(800) 258-1302

Edmund Scientific Co.
101 East Gloucester Pike
Barrington, NJ 08007
(609) 547-3488

Educational Innovations, Inc.
151 River Road
Cos Cob, CT 06807-2514
http://www.teachersource.com

Fisher Science Education
485 S. Frontage Road
Burr Ridge, IL 60521
(800) 955-4663
http://www.fisheredu.com

Frey Scientific
100 Paragon Parkway
Mansfield, OH 44903
(800) 225-3739

Nasco-Fort Atkinson
P.O. Box 901
Fort Atkinson, WI 53538-0901
(800) 558-9595

Nasco-Modesto
P.O. Box 3837
Modesto, CA 95352-3837
(800) 558-9595
http://www.nascofa.com

Sargent-Welch/VWR Scientific
P.O. Box 5229
Buffalo Grove, IL 60089-5229
(800) SAR-GENT
http://www.SargentWelch.com

Science Kit & Boreal Laboratories
777 East Park Drive
Tonawanda, NY 14150
(800) 828-7777
http://sciencekit.com

Ward's Natural Science
Establishment, Inc.
P.O. Box 92912
Rochester, NY 14692-9012
(800) 962-2660
http://www.wardsci.com

Bibliography

Ardley, Neil. *Simple Chemistry.* New York: Watts, 1985.

Beller, Joel. *So You Want to Do a Science Project.* New York: Arco, 1982.

Bombaugh, Ruth. *Science Fair Success, Revised and Expanded.* Springfield, N.J.: Enslow Publishers, Inc., 1999.

Brown, Bob. *Science For You: 112 Illustrated Experiments.* Blue Ridge Summit, Penn.: Tab Books, 1988.

———. *More Science For You: 112 Illustrated Experiments.* Blue Ridge Summit, Penn.: Tab Books, 1988.

Chishom, J., and M. Lynnington. *Chemistry.* Tulsa, Okla.: EDC, 1983.

Cobb, Vicki. *Chemically Active! Experiments You Can Do at Home.* New York: Harper & Row Jr. Books, 1985.

Corrick, James A. *Recent Revolutions in Chemistry.* New York: Watts, 1986.

Gardner, Robert. *Kitchen Chemistry.* New York: Messner, 1988.

———. *Science Around the House.* New York: Messner, 1985.

———. *Science Experiments.* New York: Watts, 1988.

Lewis, James. *Measure, Pour & Mix Kitchen Science Tricks.* New York: Meadowbrook Press, 1990.

Mebane, R. and T. R. Rybolt. *Adventures with Atoms and Molecules: Chemistry Experiments for Young People.* Hillside, N.J.: Enslow, 1985.

———. *Adventures with Atoms and Molecules. Book II*, Hillside, N.J.: Enslow, 1987.

———. *Adventures with Atoms and Molecules, Book III*. Hillside, N.J.: Enslow, 1991.

———. *Adventures with Atoms and Molecules, Book IV*. Hillside, N.J.: Enslow, 1992.

Mullin, Virginia L. *Chemistry Experiments for Children*. New York: Dover, 1968.

Tocci, Salvatore. *How to Do a Science Fair Project*. New York: Watts, 1986.

Van Cleave, Janice Pratt. *Chemistry for Every Kid: 101 Easy Experiments that Really Work*. New York: Wiley, 1989.

Van Deman, B. A., and E. MacDonald. *Nuts and Bolts: A Matter of Fact Guide to Science Fair Projects*. Harwood Heights, Ill.: Science Man Press, 1980.

Walters, Derek. *Chemistry*. New York: Watts, 1983.

Webster, David. *How to Do a Science Project*. New York: Watts, 1974.

Wertheim, J., and C. Oxlade. *Dictionary of Chemistry: All the Facts You Need to Know—At a Glance*. Tulsa, Okla.: EDC, 1987.

Internet Addresses

The World Wide Web offers access to various types of information on science projects and experiments about chemistry. In some cases you can view actual experiments or even replicate them yourself. Information is generally very current, often available without a trip to a library, and relatively easy to find.

Just as it is important to put safety first when conducting science experiments, it is also essential that you search the Web in a safe fashion and that you be critical of information you retrieve using a search engine. With over one billion indexable web sites to choose from, it is difficult to find exactly what you need and to determine that the information is reputable and authoritative. While a search engine may retrieve some useful sites, it may also overwhelm you with thousands of possibilities, many of which may be inaccurate, out-of-date, or inappropriate to your topic.

This chapter identifies and describes some of the best, most reputable, and stable sites on the web which can help you when considering doing a science project on some aspect of chemistry.

Internet Addresses researched by: Greg Byerly and Carolyn S. Brodie are Associate Professors in the School of Library and Information Science, Kent State University and write a monthly Internet column titled COMPUTER CACHE for *School Library Media Activities Monthly.*

Web Sites with Information on Chemistry

About.Com Guide to Chemistry
http://chemistry.about.com/science/chemistry/?once=true&
This About.Com site offers a constantly updated list of web resources on chemistry. The Essentials section includes links to periodic tables, conversion programs, chemical degree programs, and chemical structures archives. The best use of this site is when you have a relatively obscure chemistry topic and want to find useful web sites.

Acids and Base pH Tutorial
http://www.science.ubc.ca/~chem/tutorials/pH/launch.html
Learn the basics of acid-base chemistry by completing nineteen sections of the pH Tutor. Each section includes fairly detailed information with diagrams, formulas, and quizzes. Sections include strong acids, weak bases, buffered solutions, and acid-base indicators.

Chem4Kids

http://www.chem4kids.com/index.html

Explore five aspects of chemistry: matter, elements, atoms, math, and reactions.

Chem Team

http://dbhs.wvusd.k12.ca.us/ChemTeamIndex.html

A collection of study resources for high school and advanced placement chemistry students. Some topics include: equilibrium, radioactivity, thermo-chemistry, and kinetic molecular theory and gas laws. This site also offers a photo gallery of people and things important to chemical discoveries.

Chemicool Periodic Table

http://www.chemicool.com/

A colorful Periodic Table of the Elements with a legend that identifies each as a solid, gas, liquid or synthetic. Click on an element in the table and learn the following information: states, energies, oxidation and electrons, appearance and characteristics, reactions, other forms, conductivity, and abundance.

Chemistry Resources

http://www.dist214.k12.il.us/users/asanders/chemhome2.html

Links are provided to annotated web sites on a variety of chemistry topics, including the history of chemistry, carbon chemistry, science graphics, electronic configuration and molecular shape. Check out the project section for ideas.

Chemistry Resources

http://chem.lapeer.org/Chem1Docs/

A part of the Science Resource Center, this site offers ten demonstrations and over thirty lab investigations. Check out the rest of the site for Chemistry II and other sciences.

Chemistry Tutor

http://library.thinkquest.org/2923/index.html

This ThinkQuest site covers chemistry, basic chemistry, types of chemical reactions, laboratory tests, laws and reactions, equations, lab safety, chemical calculators, web elements, and chemistry/science links.

Chemland

http://owl.chem.umass.edu/Chemland/chemland.html

With the philosophy that students should "learn chemistry by exploring how chemical substances behave in nature," this is a highly interactive site with various chemical experiments. Topics include properties of matter, equilibia, reactivity, atomic and molecular structures, and thermodynamics.

CHEMystery
http://library.thinkquest.org/3659/
This ThinkQuest site has created a "a virtual chemistry textbook." Check out the individual chapters to find interactive resources and examples of experiments. Chapters include atoms and molecules; chemical reactions; the Periodic Table of Elements; energy; thermodynamics; equilibrium; acids and bases; organic chemistry; and nuclear reactions.

General Chemistry Online
http://antoine.frostburg.edu/chem/senese/101/
Explore this site for all of your chemistry information. The Companion Notes, Chemistry Exam Survival Guide, and FAQ are highly recommended. The glossary is very complete and even offers audio pronunciations of some terms.

HyperChemistry on the Web
http://library.thinkquest.org/2690/start.html
The site features basic chemistry concepts and dictionary definitions for over 1,000 chemistry terms. There is also a brief history of chemistry and descriptions of over 30 experiments you can do at home.

The Learning Matters of Chemistry
http://www.knowledgebydesign.com/tlmc/tlmc.html
An interactive site with models and computer animations of famous experiments. Check out computer graphics for visualizations of molecular models and atomic orbitals. There are various online exercises, as well as downloadable computer-aided learning programs.

High School Chemistry
http://schmidel.com/hub/chem.htm
This site from High School Hub provides links to general chemistry sites, periodical tables, information on molecular structures, and chemical references. It also includes laboratory experiments, questions, quizzes, and matching games.

The pHFactor
http://www.miamisci.org/ph/
Learn about acids, bases, and pH factor by exploring the seven E's: excite, explore, explain, expand, extend, exchange, and examine. Each section contains a variety of activities and educational experiences.

SMILE Program Chemistry Index
http://www.iit.edu/~smile/cheminde.html
Features over 200 single concept lessons relating to chemistry. Some lessons include basic tools and principles, atomic and molecular structure, states of matter, types and control of chemical reactions and chemistry of elements, and compounds and materials.

Understanding Our Planet Through Chemistry
http://minerals.cr.usgs.gov/gips/aii-home.htm
This site by the U.S. Geological Survey "shows how chemists and geologists use analytical chemistry to determine the age of the Earth; show that an extraterrestrial body collided with the Earth; predict volcanic eruptions; observe atmospheric change over millions of years; and document damage by acid rain and pollution of the Earth's surface."

Wilton High School Chemistry
http://www.chemistrycoach.com/home.htm
This site is one of the best sites designed and maintained by high school chemistry students. Especially helpful are the collection of original tutorials and the extensive list of links to other chemical tutorials and study skills. There is even information on chemistry-related careers.

Science Fairs

Science Fair Central
http://school.discovery.com/sciencefaircentral/
Part of the Discovery Channel School site, Science Fair Central is a great place to begin researching a science project. The Science Fair Studio includes a detailed handbook on the steps in a science project which is based on the print publication, *A Guide to the Best Science Fair Projects*, by Janice VanCleave. Check out Jake's Attic which features a different experiment each month.

Science Fair Projects Index
http://www.ascpl.lib.oh.us/scifair/sftp.htm
This site is an electronic database prepared by the Akron-Summit County (OH) Public Library of science fair projects which have been included in books dating from 1990 to the present. Since the books must be consulted to get further information about the projects, this site is best used when trying to pick a topic or to see if your idea has already been done. The projects may be searched by subject, experiment title or grade level.

SciFair.org

http://www.scifair.org

Also known as the Ultimate Science Fair Resource, this site includes articles on project steps, project hints, the scientific method, writing reports, and display boards. You can use the Idea Bank to brainstorm about possible topics and then share your ideas with others on the Idea Board.

Your Science Fair Project Resource Guide

http://www.ipl.org/youth/projectguide/

This instructional guide from the Internet Public Library covers: choosing a topic, sample projects, resources, and ask an expert. Basic information is provided and accompanied by links to other science-related sites.

General Science Web Sites

Bill Nye the Science Guy's Nye Labs Online

http://nyelabs.kcts.org/

This is the online lab for this popular TV show. Bill Nye, the Science Guy, makes science fun, but he also suggests real experiments and projects you can try at home.

Exploratorium

http://www.exploratorium.edu/

The Exploratorium is an online "museum of science, art, and human perception." Search the archives to find collections of past exhibitions, digital images, archived webcasts, and webcam sites. The Exploratorium is best known for its cow's eye dissection, but it includes many other interactive science activities.

Math & Science Gateway

http://www.tc.conell.edu/Edu/MathSciGateway/

This comprehensive site provides "links to resources in mathematics and science for educators and students in grades 9–12." Subjects covered include biology, chemistry, the environment, health, mathematics, and physics.

The Science Page

http://www.sciencepage.org/

Another good collection of science and science education sites which can be used to research a wide range of science topics: weather, chemistry, physics, and biology. Check out the science fair projects and the activities, labs, and lesson plans. A unique aspect of the site is its collection of science analogies.

Index